TIME TRAM DUNDEE

TIME TRAM DUNDEE

A JOURNEY THROUGH THE HISTORY OF DUNDEE

BY MATTHEW FITT
ILLUSTRATED BY KEITH ROBSON

WAVERLEY
BOOKS

Published 2006 for Dundee City Council by Waverley Books,
an imprint of Geddes & Grosset, David Dale House,
New Lanark, Scotland ML11 9DJ.

www.dundeecity.gov.uk/timetram

Time Tram Dundee

Acknowledgements

Dundee City Council gratefully acknowledges the support of the Heritage Lottery Fund.

Moira Foster, Stuart Syme, and Lynn Moy, who managed this project, would like to thank all those who have supported this initiative, especially the children of Dundee.

Thanks also to Louise Yeoman, Sheila Hawkins, Iain Flett and the Local Studies Department of Dundee Central Library.

Where on Earth is Dundee?

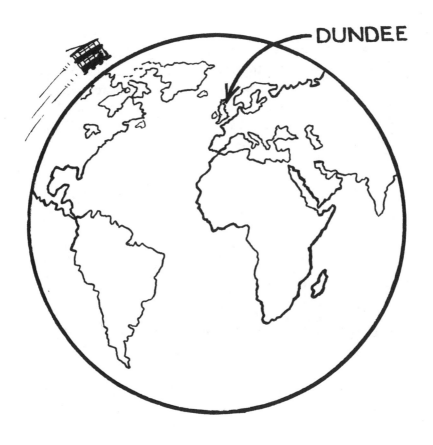

DUNDEE

All Aboard For Dundee...

The city of Dundee sits at the mouth of the River Tay and it's been sitting there a very long time.

Over the centuries, hundreds of thousands of people have come to Dundee, some to make their fortune, others to make a nuisance of themselves. Some turned up and knocked everything down while some made sacks, newspapers and a few million jars of marmalade. Most were ordinary folk that just got on with it and made Dundee their home.

With all those people who've lived, breathed and died in the same town, Dundee is wriggling and crawling and groaning with history. It's a place full of stories bursting to get out there and be told.

Just as well the Time Tram's ready to leave on a special new route round the history of Dundee. And there are a few friendly characters on board who'll tell you all about the happy, sad, daft but definitely exciting things that have happened in this historic city.

Mr Scrymgeour, he's your driver. Young Davie is on hand to punch your tickets so please have them ready. Eh Ken the Seagate seagull is coming along for the ride to keep everyone right and to get up old Scrymgeour's nose. And if you hurry there's a seat on the Dundee Time Tram waiting just for you.

Dundee Now

Today Dundee is Scotland's fourth largest city and 150,000 people live by 59.30N, 2.58W on the north bank of the Firth of Tay.

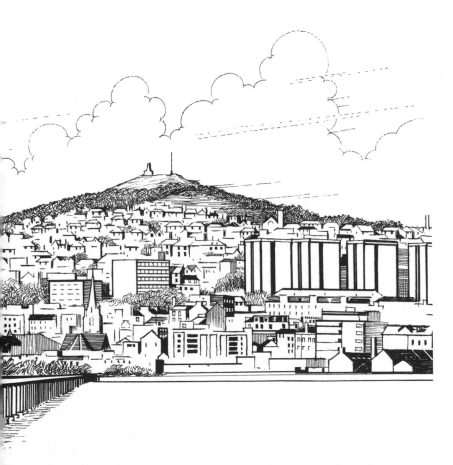

Dundee has 30,000 students, 1,400 hours of sunshine a year, 800 years of burgh history, 59 parks, 7 twin towns, 2 professional football teams, 2 bridges, 2 cathedrals, 2 universities, 1 medieval tower, 1 statue of Desperate Dan and 1 dead volcano.

Dundee in 1881

The jute industry brought thousands of people to Dundee. In 1801, there were 26,000 Dundonians. By 1881, the population was already 140,000.

The city had 50,000 mill workers, 700 whalers, 125 mills, 85 churches, 5 docks, 3 railway stations and half a bridge.

Dundee 500 years ago

About 500 years ago, Dundee was a prosperous town with a population of over 5,000.

Dundee had mansion houses, markets, monasteries and the largest church tower in the land. Its people made cloth, hats, gloves and guns and traded their goods with cities in Holland, Germany, England, France and Russia.

Dundee 1,000 years ago

Around 1,000 years ago, Dundee was a small fishing village on the north shore of the River Tay.

The people lived in the Seagate close to St Nicholas' Craig and Black Rock.

They had 2 rocks, 2 burns, 1 river, 1 street and all the fish they could eat.

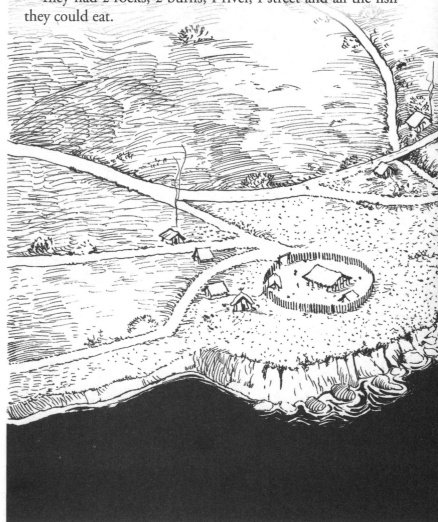

Dundee, Way Way Back

Way way back in time, about 12,000 years ago at the end of the last Ice Age, there wasn't much to see in Dundee.

ice ↗   ↖snaa

Dundee was covered in ice, hundreds of feet of the stuff. For thousands of years, gigantic chunks of frozen water called glaciers had been rumbling slowly across the top of it.

Sometimes two miles high, the glaciers over time dug a huge long trench out of the earth. When they melted, the trench filled with water, forming the natural wonder that makes Dundee truly bonnie – the River Tay.

Dundee, Way Way Even Further Back

Way way even further back in time, about 470,000,000 years ago, Dundee wasn't in the same place it is now.

Scotland lay south of the Equator joined to North America on one enormous supercontinent called Laurentia.

Over millions of years, forces inside the Earth shuffled the land around like a pack of cards.

Finally Laurentia split apart. North America went one way and Scotland went the other, drifting very slowly over to where it is today.

A Hill in the Huff

These days it's perfectly safe to go up Dundee Law. You can lay out your tartan rug and have a picnic on the grass. As you eat your Keiller's marmalade pieces, you can listen to the birds, enjoy the view and think what a quiet peaceful place it is. You might even want to just shut your eyes and have a nap.

But 400,000,000 years ago, Dundee Law wasn't all that peaceful and it certainly wasn't quiet....

23

Dundee Law Goes Doolally

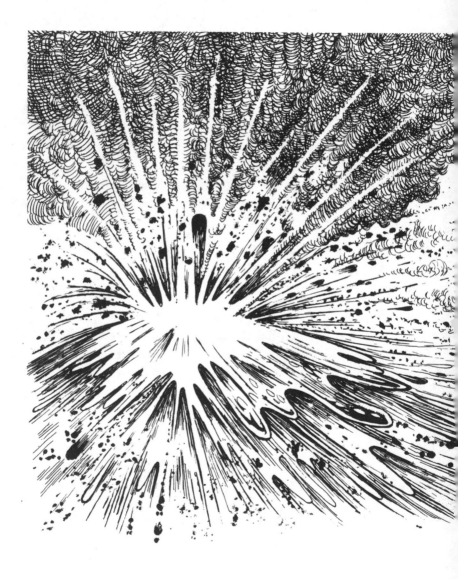

Dundee Law was once a volcano with a foul temper. Put it in a bad mood and the Law would blow its top, throwing out rivers of molten lava and making the land round about shoogle like jelly on a plate.

Luckily for modern Dundonians, the Law is extinct and highly unlikely to go off again any time soon. The hill we can see today isn't even the actual volcano.

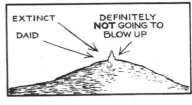

EXTINCT
DAID

DEFINITELY **NOT** GOING TO BLOW UP

The original mountain was much bigger. Dundee Law is just the plug. This means it's the tiny little bit of very hard rock left over after the huge volcano had belched out all its nastiness and blown itself to pieces. The Law (which is a Scots word for 'hill') is a fine place to go for a gentle stroll but this 571 foot high ex-volcano has played an active part in Dundee's history.

It once had a fort. A Jacobite rebellion was launched from its summit. And at one time, a railway line ran right through the middle of it.

PHEW! EH'M MELTIN'

Are we going any further back into the past, Mr. Scrymgeour?

DON'T WORRY LAD THIS IS AS FAR BACK AS THE TRAM GOES

TIME TRAM

Next stop, Prehistoric Dundee

A Tale of Two Rocks

Prehistoric Dundee

MESOLITHIC MIDDENS

About 8,000 years ago, the first people moved into the area around Dundee.

Nowadays we call them the Mesolithic people and these Mesolithic folk had only one thought in their heads – food and how to get hold of it.

WHY DUNDEE?

N⁰ CRABBIT VOLCANOES
N⁰ GLACIERS TO
LICK AND GET YOUR
TONGUE STUCK ON.
N⁰ NOISY NEIGHBOURS

★ NOSH ★

With the volcanoes dead and the ice all melted, Scotland was the place to go for a bite to eat. Its rivers like the Tay were full of fish and the deer in its forests had never heard of a bow and arrow. To the small bands of hunters drifting up from the south, the land around Dundee was one big dinner time.

Long before Dundee was even called Dundee, the first people, also known as Hunter-Gatherers, were busy doing mainly two things – hunting and gathering.

27

Old rubbish? Exactly. That's how we know the Mesolithic people were here. When the railway to Aberdeen was being built in the 1800s, workers found an 8,000 year old midden (or rubbish heap) on the shoreline at the Stannergate between Dundee and Broughty Ferry.

A midden was where people flung the bones of the poor animal they'd just scoffed

The Big Flit

But the Stannergate was cold. The wind was always wrecking folk's hairdos and blowing up their animal skin kilts. The people needed a less blowy place to live. A couple of miles to the west up the River Tay they came across a spot sheltered from the elements by two rocks.

Black Rock and St Nicholas' Craig

Now a rock is just a big lump of stone and usually nothing to shout about. But it's from Black Rock and St Nicholas' Craig that the history of Dundee really gets going.

You would have a hard job seeing these two rocks today because a great big modern city has been built on top of them.

And the original shoreline isn't easy to spot either. Landfill (great chunks of earth and stone bunged into the sea) has over the years pushed the town further out into the river. It's all safe and solid ground now but if you'd been walking thousands of years ago along the line of much of today's seafront, you might have got your trainers a bit wet.

solid grund

WHA'S STOLE THE PAVIE?

SPLASH!

Naturally Dundee

When the River Tay was in a foul mood, the folk found protection from the rough water beside the Black Rock and St Nicholas' Craig. There the people could fish and swim and wash their armpits without fear of being walloped by the waves.

And they'd stumbled across the best natural harbour on the whole east coast of Scotland.

Scotland was a land of plenty. Plenty deer to bump on the head and have for your tea. Plenty fresh water to guzzle. Plenty room to live in peace and quiet. Word must have got out that life in Dundee was so good.

Around 4000 BC a new lot, the Neolithic people, started arriving from Europe. They brought with them new tools, new animals and a crafty new way of getting hold of food – farming.

FUN THINGS YOU CAN DO WITH STONE

The Neolithic farmers didn't have to run after wild pigs all day and so had more time to think. Unfortunately it's quite hard to tell what they were thinking. Today we can jot our ideas down on paper but the Neolithic people couldn't. Paper (*and* writing) hadn't reached Scotland yet. Instead Neolithic folk used dirty great lumps of stone.

dirty great lump of stone

Cup and ring marks were found on a stone in the Earth House at Tealing. What sort of people would carve circles onto stone?

31

Some stones may have marked holy places. A stone known as the Druid (or holy man) stands on one of the fairways on the golf course at Camperdown Park.

The ancient stone circle at Balgarthno is still standing to this day. Why do you think the Stone Age Dundonians built it?

Bronze Age Dundee

The secret of how to make bronze reached Scotland around the year 2000 BC. (Showing off was invented round about the same time.)

The Bronze Age people had an unusual way of burying their dead. In the old days, a whole lot of dead folk were piled together in a chamber called a barrow. (Sometimes they stripped the flesh from the bodies first.)

The new Bronze Age custom was to bury the dead in a single grave. Food and jewels were left beside the body to help the soul on its journey in the after-life.

The Wyntoun Barrow found near Dundee

Farmers dug up a grave like this one near Forfar

Iron Age Dundee

The coming of the Iron Age made a huge difference to folk's lives. It meant they could make really sharp things out of iron and then stick them into each other.

More tribes moved in, looking for good farmland to settle on. But more folk and less land soon added up to less food and more trouble. And when there was every chance your neighbour might come round to bop you on the head and steal your best cow, stronger swords and sharper spears quickly became extremely popular.

The Dundee Dragon

Long, long ago, in the valley of Strathmartine not far from Dundee, it is said there lived a farmer who had nine daughters. One day he asked his eldest daughter to fetch water from the well. The girl obediently left to get the water but didn't come home.

So the farmer sent his second eldest daughter to the well but she didn't come back either.

The farmer sent his third daughter, his fourth, his fifth… to cut a sorry tale short, the farmer sent each of his nine daughters to the well to fetch water and not one of them came home.

He couldn't think what was taking them so long. Finally he got off his backside and went down to get the water himself. But what he saw there made him throw up his hands in horror.

35

A dragon was sitting by the well holding its belly and burping loudly. Nine empty buckets lay round about. The beast had eaten all nine maidens.

The farmer ran to tell the other men of the village. Among them was a young man called Martin who was in love with one of the lassies.

braa cuddie

TAK THAT YA BRUTE!

daid drag

Martin chased the dragon across the hills at the back of Dundee. Close to Baldragon, he caught the beast and slew it.

Dundee's Modern Dragons

The dragon in the old Dundee legend came to a sticky end but if you look closely you'll still see the odd dragon lurking about in the modern city. There are two on Dundee's coat-of-arms and you might even find one among the Saturday shoppers in the Murraygate.

'With thought and purity'

Run to the Hill

Dragons weren't the Iron Age people's biggest worry though. It was the folk round about them that they really had to keep an eye on.

Whenever hairy thugs from a neighbouring tribe came to town, the locals tended to run straight up the nearest hill to escape a thumping.

The people of ancient Dundee were luckier than most. In more or less everyone's back garden stood a rather large hill, the Law. And to make doubly sure the raiders couldn't touch them (or their cattle), they built a large wooden fort at the top of it.

37

Dundee Diary, 100 BC

Nechtan, aged 10

The hound lifts his head. He sniffs. He shows his white teeth and growls.

I hear them now. My brother hears them too. We listen to the horses' hooves on the ground. We can't see them but we know they are coming. We have heard horses carrying men with heavy swords and shields before.

Across the glen, the people on the Balgay Hill have seen what we have heard. They put wet straw on their fires to make smoke to warn us.

We pick up our fishing nets and run as the dark smoke rises into the sky.

Everyone is running. Women drive their cattle and sheep and scream at the animals to move faster. Old women gather up bairns in their arms and children help the oldest folk to climb the hill. My brother and I overtake our sister and her friends. We run with the men up the slopes of the Law.

I am tired when we reach the fort. I rest my shoulder against the fort's outer wall. Its wood is rough and scratches my skin. I look down at the hillside over the heads of my sister and my mother dragging the cattle over the heather. Far below, a hundred men on horses are splashing through the burn where my brother and I fished all afternoon.

One of the older boys pushes me. He shouts at me to hurry. I shout back but he is already through the gate. I follow and see my father carrying bundles of arrows under his arm. His face is red. He calls to me to help him. He gives me a bundle of arrows and we climb the wall of the fort.

The day is calm but beyond the river I see rain falling on the land. Inside the fort, people are running with their arms full of stones. The last time the horsemen came from the north my father made me bring stones to the wall for the older boys to throw.

Men with bows and arrows stand on the wall. My father talks to each one, slapping them on the shoulder. When he comes to me, he puts his bow in my hand. He does not slap my shoulder. He points to the line of men and horses moving towards the foot of the hill through the long yellow grass. I take the bow and put an arrow to it. I draw back the bowstring and wait.

41

Romans, Picts and Scots

Roman Dundee

While Dundee was still just a hill-fort and folk were busy throwing stones at each other, some people in Italy had already built themselves a city. The city was called Rome.

The Romans didn't bother pinching pigs and cows. They put together the biggest army the world had ever seen and pinched other people's countries instead. By the year 40 AD, the Roman Empire stretched from Africa to the north of England.

The Roman army invaded Scotland in 84 AD and had lots of punch-ups with the local tribes. They won most of their battles but the Romans never completely conquered the land they called Caledonia.

The outline of Roman marching camps can still be seen near Dundee at Longforgan, Invergowrie and Clatto. In these camps the foot-sore Roman legionaries could rest their weary tootsies and give their blisters a good squeeze before marching back into the hills to beat up more Caledonians.

The Romans had a nickname for the tough painted warriors of the north-east of Scotland. The nickname stuck and to this day we use the same name. The Romans called these warriors Picts.

The Picts in Dundee

When the Romans left in 380 AD, Scotland was divided into four main regions. The biggest of these regions was known as Pictland which stretched from the River Forth as far north as Orkney and Shetland. Although Dundee is now Scottish, 1,500 years ago it lay deep in the heartland of the Picts.

The Picts were a family of Celtic-speaking tribes who ruled the northern lands for 500 years. Not much is known about the Picts but some say that they were descendants of the very first settlers.

The big thing to know about the Picts is that they painted their bodies to scare the wits out of their enemies in battle.

The Picts were brave warriors. When Dundee was a Pictish settlement, its people would have spent much of their day doing combat training. They carved pictures of their battles and lives onto great tall stones which still stand in fields all around Dundee.

Maybe it was because the land of the Picts was rich and fertile, or perhaps people were jealous of their great skill at carving stones.

Or maybe with all those tattoos on their gubs, the other tribes thought they were making faces at them. Whatever the reason, during the Dark Ages the Picts in the lands around Dundee had many enemies.

The Picts' Enemies

The Angles: rude hairy brutes from the north of England.

The Scots: a squad of tough, short-tempered desperados from Ireland.

The Britons: grim, unwashed bruisers from the south of Scotland.

The Vikings: pushy, bloodthirsty butchers from Scandinavia.

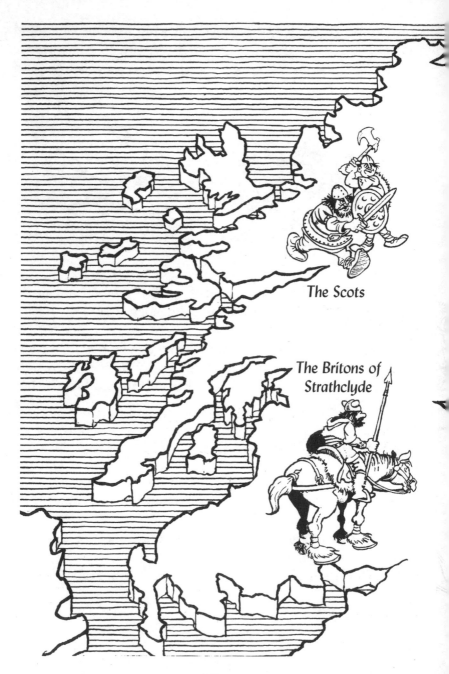

The Scots

The Britons of
Strathclyde

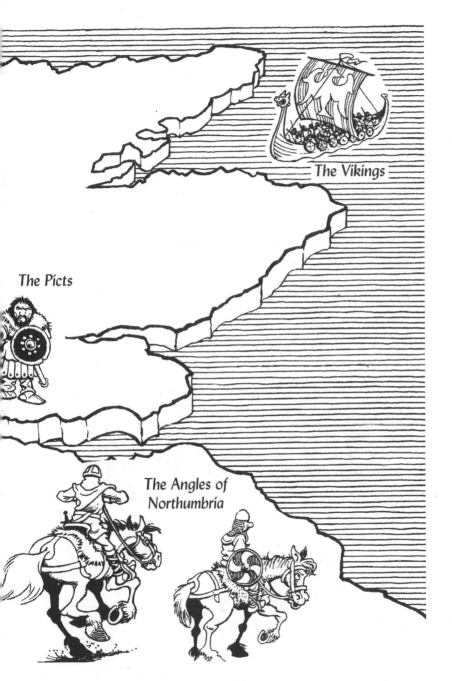

The Vikings

The Picts

The Angles of
Northumbria

Christianity Comes to Dundee

St Columba was a famous Irish missionary who didn't think twice about crossing raging seas in a tiny boat or standing up to huffy kings or chieftains. Once, it's said, he even put a monster in its place.

In 563 AD, Columba sailed by coracle across the Irish Sea to Scotland. He landed on the windswept island of Iona and built a draughty monastery. From Iona, Columba planned to turn the grimy Godless peoples of Scotland into good God-fearing Christians.

Some folk were Christians already, converted by a saint called Ninian. But before Columba came along, it wasn't unusual to find people worshipping trees or wells or even praying to the sun.

Columba got on fine with the Scots because he was Irish just like them. He soon converted the west and turned his attention to the Scots' arch enemy, the Picts. The journey into Pictland was dangerous. The locals might kill him as soon as look at him. But when he saved one of them from the clutches of a water monster near Inverness, the Pictish king shook him by the hand and made him a guest of honour. Columba travelled through

Pictland, preaching to them about Christianity. It is said that he converted a group of Picts on the Carse of Gowrie between Perth and Dundee.

THE BATTLE OF NECHTANSMERE

Even a century after the death of Columba, Scotland wasn't yet called Scotland. The Angle tribes of the south had put together a powerful empire called Northumbria. Under King Egfrith, the Angles had thumped the Britons, Scots and Picts

50

a few times already and by 685 AD they thought they could push everyone around.

But on the 20th of May that year, a battle was fought near Dundee that sorted out the Angles once and for all and shaped the nation we now call Scotland.

Near Dunnichen a few miles from Forfar, the Picts drew the invading Northumbrian army into battle on the soft soggy ground of a field called Nechtansmere. The Pictish king Bridei waited until the Angles were stuck in the mud and then attacked with all his men.

The Battle of Nechtansmere was basically a mud bath followed by a blood bath. King Egfrith was slain and the Angles who weren't trampled into the ground were enslaved by the Picts.

Alpin and Son

It is said that in the Dark Ages another savage battle was fought between the Scots and the Picts at King's Cross, near the town's present-day Kingsway. Legend tells that the Picts captured Alpin, the Scottish king, and cut his head off on Dundee Law.

The Picts and the Scots were a funny lot, pals one minute, lopping each other's heads off the next.

Often they fought side by side against wild Viking invaders but most of the time they were at each other's throats.

In 844 AD, Alpin's son, Kenneth MacAlpin, became King of Scots.

Under MacAlpin, the Scots and the Picts joined together for good. The two peoples were united and the country of Scotland was born.

Dundee was now officially Scottish. And in the coming centuries, it would rise to be one of the most important towns in the new Scottish nation.

How Dundee Got Its Name

Dundee was not always called Dundee.

The Romans, when they had booted the Picts out of their hill-fort on the Law named it **Taodunum**, meaning 'fort on the Tay'.

And the Picts who got their hill back when the Romans left called the settlement **Alec** which was an old Celtic word for 'beautiful'.

Even as late as the Middle Ages, it was still sometimes known as **Alectum** which translates as the 'beautiful place' or 'Bonnie Dundee'.

The word **Dundee** was written down for the first time about 1,000 years ago. It appeared in a Charter for another Scottish town in 1054. (A Charter is a very important piece of paper.)

V. important
piece of
paper

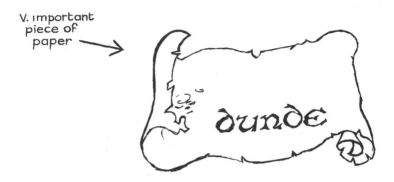

But Dundee must have been a famous place even then because around the same time someone carved its name into a stone as far away as Denmark.

You may have noticed that in the past the word 'Dundee' could be spelled a couple of different ways. In fact all sorts of spellings were in use until the 19th century when it was agreed it should be DUNDEE (which is how you should always spell it or you'll look extremely silly).

Dunde...Dundeo...
Dude...Dundee..Donde
Don...Dun... Dude?

But What Does It Actually Mean

Dun~

The first part is easy. 'Dun' is Gaelic for 'hill' or 'fort on a hill'. It turns up in names such as Dunbar, Dunfermline, Dunkeld, Dunedin and of course in Dundee Cake.

'Dee' is the tricky bit. No-one is completely sure what it means. Here are a few of the ideas people have come up with over the years. Which one do you think might be right?

~dee

Dundee, Hill of Fire: The Law is a great spot for lighting fires to warn of an attack (or to let everyone know it's your birthday). Some think the name means 'fire'.

Dundee, Gift of God: Some say the name comes from the Latin 'Dei donum ' which means God's Gift.

MERRY CHRISTMAS

56

Dundee, A Hill belonging to a Guy called Diag: Diag, a local chief, used to be the top banana in Dundee. Some believe the town is named after him.

Dundee, Hill at the River Mouth: Some reckon that long ago the town was called **Dundeo**. 'Deo' is an old Gaelic word for river mouth.

But maybe it's much less complicated than all that.

One old spelling of the town's name was **Duntay** and it could be that Dundee simply means 'Hill-fort on the Tay'.

57

Dundee Gets Its First Street

If you were a visitor to Dundee in the year 1000, you would have found a harbour, a wooden fort, one or two huts and that was about it. Dundee then was not much more than a good place to catch fish.

Dundee, one thousand years ago

Earl David's Town

During the 11th century, a row of huts sprang up along the shoreline to the east of Black Rock. People walked past these rough shacks every day to get to the harbour. They stopped to have a chinwag.

Shops opened.

More people moved in.

New huts were built. Dundee's first street, the Seagate, had begun to appear.

DUNDEE'S FIRST STREET WAS A ROAD TO THE SEA. THAT'S WHAT THE WORD 'SEAGATE' (SOMETIMES 'SEAGAIT') MEANS

The Seagate used to be right at the water's edge

SOME O MEH BEST PALS BIDE DOON THE SEAGATE

Nowadays cars and buses hurry along the Seagate. No-one seems to notice it very much in the rush to get home or go shopping but the Seagate, which used to stand right at the river's edge, is more than a thousand years old. That makes it the oldest street in Dundee.

Dundee's Two Burns

troot

Like the two rocks which sheltered Dundee from the sea, there were two burns which supplied its people with fresh running water. These two streams, the Scouringburn and the Dens Burn, rose in the hills behind Dundee and ran down into the sea at either end of the Seagate.

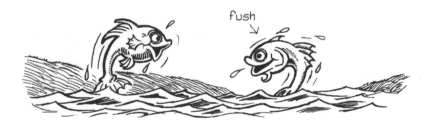

fush

The Scouringburn and the Dens were used by the townsfolk for drinking and washing and then later by industry. They are now hidden below the city streets but many times in the town's history, Dundee's burns ran red with blood.

And whenever important men were scratching each other's eyes out for control of Scotland, Dundee always seemed to end up right in the thick of it.

Malcolm Canmore in Dundee

In 1054, it was the turn of Malcolm Canmore and King Macbeth to slog it out.

Macbeth had bumped off Malcolm's grandfather and now Malcolm wanted revenge.

Malcolm was with his army in Dundee when he learned that Macbeth's soldiers were gathering near Perth. Leaping onto his horse, Malcolm Canmore rode out of Dundee on the way to fight the famous battle of Dunsinane.

𝕰𝕳! **Magazine's Royal Wedding of the Year, 1070**

All eyes are on Dundee this year as Scotland celebrates the royal wedding of King Malcolm Canmore and Queen Margaret.

THE GROOM

Malcolm Canmore

He's tough. He's handsome. His name means Big Head. Malcolm III finally tracked down his old enemy Macbeth and murdered him. In 1057, he became King of Scots. Malcolm's hobbies include plundering, invading England and the occasional quiet game of chess.

THE BRIDE

Queen Margaret

Glamorous bride Margaret (25) is a true fairy tale princess. Born in Hungary, Margaret is the daughter of an English king, she is currently on the run from William the Conqueror. In her spare time she likes building churches, founding monasteries, helping the poor and nagging the Scots to go to church more often.

ЄᏂ! **Exclusive Sketches of the Happy Couple**

Eh! Magazine brings you the first sketches of the opening of Whitehall Palace which King Malcolm built in Dundee for his blushing bride, Queen Margaret.

Earl David of Huntingdon

At the start of the 12th century, Dundee was a one-street wonder. By that century's end, it had changed from a no bad place to buy fish into a busy market town. And the man who got things moving was a nobleman called David.

His full title was Earl David of Huntingdon and he was not short of friends in high places. His grandfather, also called David, was king of Scotland and both his brothers, Malcolm and William, became king too.

David and his brother, William the Lion, must have been really good pals because the king was forever giving him presents of new bits of land. One morning, Earl David woke up to find he was the proud owner of Dundee.

David had big plans to put Dundee on the map. He laid out new streets and built a stone castle on Black Rock. At the same time, he was doing up the harbour to make it safe

Earl David
1174–1219

64

for foreign merchant ships to come in to trade and hand over great big wads of money. Dundee and Earl David soon grew rich together.

And not long after, the people of Dundee got some really good news. Dundee was to become a Burgh.

How to Turn a Town into a Burgh in Three Easy Steps

Step 1 – First you need a town. Any town will do but it's better if it's one that's got buckets of cash rolling in.

Step 2 – Next you need a big cheese, maybe a king, to notice your town and like what you're doing with the place. (It's always handy if the king happens to be your brother.)

Step 3 (and this is crucial) – Get the king to grant your town a Charter.

Congratulations, your town is now a Burgh. This means you have the right to hold markets whenever you fancy and collect taxes from the other towns round about (which isn't very fair on them but great for you). Dundee, thanks to Earl David, was made a Burgh in 1191.

The Legends of Earl David

Over the years, a couple of tall tales have turned up about Earl David and the things he was supposed to have done. The first one is that he might have been Robin Hood's dad.

The second one is a bit more complicated and tells the story of how St Mary's Church, the oldest kirk in Dundee, came to be built.

David, so the legend says, was on a Crusade in the Holy Land when he was captured by the locals. When they learned that he was royalty, they gave him a boat to sail back to Scotland. But off Norway, his ship was caught in a terrible storm.

David, thinking his number was up, prayed to God to bring him safely home. In return he promised that wherever he landed he would build a church to the Virgin Mary. David landed in Dundee and founded St Mary's. The original church no longer exists but a kirk with the same name stands to this day on the same spot in the centre of Earl David's town.

Devorguilla's Monastery

Earl David's granddaughter (who went by the really unusual name of Devorguilla) established Greyfriars' Monastery in Dundee about 1260.

Earl Davie's 'Dev'

Dundee 1286, A Successful Burgh

1286, no invasions (yet)

Dundee in the Wars

Bad News for Dundee

In 1286, Dundee was a prosperous burgh. Ten years later, it was a smoking ruin.

It all started to go wrong in March 1286 when King Alexander III of Scotland tumbled over a cliff at Kinghorn in Fife while out riding his horse on a wild winter's night.

heh
cliff

It was bad news for King Alexander as it was a very high cliff and the fall killed him. But it was double bad news for Scotland because Alexander had died with no heir to come after him.

The only hope lay in his three-year-old granddaughter but when she died in Orkney on her way over from Norway, it was triple bad news for Scotland and Dundee.

John Balliol and Robert Bruce started shouting very loudly that they should be the next King of Scotland. Both were descended from Dundee's very own Earl David of Huntingdon, and Devorguilla (who founded Greyfriars' Monastery) was John Balliol's mum.

In the end, the two men agreed that King Edward I of England should choose the next king.

Edward I of England's Visit to Dundee

Edward I's nickname was 'Hammer of the Scots' because he enjoyed nothing better than visiting Scotland and hammering Scottish folk. So letting someone with a nickname like that pick the future king of Scotland was bound to end in tears sooner or later.

Edward I chose John Balliol. To pay him back Balliol had to let Edward tell him what to do. But then Balliol got a little too friendly with England's sworn enemy, the French. Edward, who reckoned Scotland belonged to him anyway, kicked John Balliol out of his job and nabbed the Scottish crown for himself. Then Edward came north with his army (and his hammer) to show his new subjects who was boss.

On his visit to Dundee in August 1296, he got his soldiers to beat up the people and set fire to the town.

There's Invasion No 1

Some folk hid in St Mary's Church hoping the English king would not harm them in God's House. Edward didn't really care whose house it was and burned the kirk down anyway with everyone still inside.

On and off for about the next twenty years, Scotland was under English rule, its castles and towns stuffed with English soldiers and noblemen, like Selbie, the governor of Dundee. The Scots didn't like it one little bit.

The English governor, Selbie, gets his first taste of a Dundee peh

A rebellion broke out, led by a man called William Wallace which soon turned into a long desperate struggle for freedom known as the Wars of Independence. And there is a story told by the medieval writer, Blind Harry, that it all got started in Dundee's Seagate.

William Wallace in Dundee

William Wallace was a pupil at Dundee Grammar School. On the way to school one day, he was attacked in the Seagate by the English governor's son. Wallace fought back, killing young Selbie in the brawl.

Fleeing to his uncle's house, he was hidden by his aunt who dressed him up like an old woman. If the English caught him, they would execute him on the spot.

Wallace managed to slip out of Dundee but spent many years living as a fugitive from the soldiers of King Edward I.

But in 1297, history tells us that William Wallace came to Dundee at the head of a Scottish rebel army and laid siege to the English garrison in Dundee Castle. Wallace had to leave at half-time to fight the Battle of Stirling Bridge (which he won) and when he got back to Dundee, the English soldiers quickly surrendered.

A year later, while Wallace wasn't looking, the English sneaked back into Dundee Castle. A second siege began but Wallace had to leave at half-time again to face Edward I at the Battle of Falkirk (which he lost).

Wallace left a Dundonian called Alexander Carron in charge of the siege and with a force of 8,000 Scots he pulverised the English garrison and most of Dundee Castle into the bargain.

The Skirmisher

Carron was nicknamed the Skirmisher because he was a brave fighter and liked a good scrap. 'Skirmisher' became the surname 'Scrymgeour'.

Wallace made Scrymgeour the Constable of Dundee and granted him lands at Dudhope where his family built a castle. And though it meant the enemy tried extra hard to kill him, he was also given the great honour of carrying the Scottish flag into battle.

Dudhope Castle as it looks today

The Scrymgeours were still battling centuries later. In 1922, Edwin (or Neddy) Scrymgeour won a famous victory over Winston Churchill in the General Election to become Member of Parliament for Dundee.

'Neddy' Scrymgeour
1866–1947

Winston Churchill
1874–1965

Edward I's Second Visit to Dundee

Edward I, fed up of all the rebellions, paid Scotland another visit in 1303 to remind the Scots that he was still their lord and master. He invaded Dundee again in June with a good mind to burn the town down, forgetting he had already torched it the first time.

Edward's soldiers finally caught up with the Scottish rebel leaders. William Wallace was hanged, drawn and quartered in London in 1305. And bold Alexander Carron the Skirmisher had his neck stretched in Newcastle the following year.

Robert the Bruce in Dundee

Robert the Bruce, who took up the struggle for freedom after Wallace, was confirmed as King of Scotland in 1309 in Devorguilla's Monastery of the Greyfriars in Dundee.

Edward I had since died and his son, Edward II, was no match for King Robert.

The Scots recaptured Dundee Castle for the last time in 1313 and demolished it to make sure the English couldn't use it again.

And in 1314, Robert the Bruce led the Scots to victory over the English in a field near Stirling called Bannockburn.

Scotland and Dundee were free of English occupation (at least for a while).

The Ups and Downs of Dundee Castle

1191

From earliest times, a small wooden fort stood on Black Rock defending the harbour. In the 12th century, Earl David built a stone castle on the same spot overlooking his new burgh.

1296

1297

When Edward I put Selbie in charge of Dundee Castle, it was no less than William Wallace who brought it back into Scottish hands. And when it was grabbed again for England, the Constable of Dundee, Alexander Scrymgeour promptly snatched it back for Scotland.

1298

1298

1303   1303

Each time it was captured by either the Scots or the English, the Castle took a pasting. When it was occupied again by the English in 1303, they fixed its walls. But in 1313, the Scots captured the Castle and, fearing more invasions by the English, knocked it down themselves.

1313   1314

For centuries after its demolition, it stood as a ruin on Castle Hill. 540 years later, St Paul's Cathedral was built on the rock. The fortress is remembered in the name Castle Street. If you look really closely at the base of the Cathedral, you can still see bits of the original Black Rock.

Cannibals and Pirates

Medieval Dundee

Dundee After Edward I

The Wars of Independence left Dundee in a right old mess.

The first thing it required though was not wood or stones as you might expect. In those days a burgh needed something far more important – a piece of paper.

Remember the special piece of paper William the Lion gave Dundee to turn it into a burgh in 1191? Well, Edward I nicked it. So in 1327 to help the town get back on its feet, King Robert the Bruce gave Dundee a brand new Charter.

← brand new v. important piece of paper

THIS CHARTER IS STILL IN THE CITY ARCHIVE

You mean we can go and look at something from 1327?

JIST LOOK AT SCRYMGEOUR HE'S MUCH AALDER THAN THAT

Robert the Bruce's Charter restored Dundee's old rights to trade freely, hold markets and generally make money again. The king also gave the go-ahead for the town to build itself a **Tolbooth**.

The Tolbooth was one of the most important buildings in the burgh but it was not the most popular. It's where you went to pay your tolls or taxes. And if you broke the law, the Tolbooth would be where you'd get locked up.

Dundee's first Tolbooth was built in 1325

For hundreds of years, Dundee's **Mercat Cross** stood at the heart of burgh life.

The Cross was meant to be a quiet place for holy thoughts but folk mostly stood round it, catching up on gossip and selling pies.

Going in through the door and climbing a little stair, the Provost would announce news about wars, kings and national events to crowds of Dundonians eager to hear what was going on in the world.

Dundee's first Mercat Cross was built in the Seagate in the 14th century. It was then moved to the Marketgate in the later Middle Ages.

A new Cross was built in 1586. Pieces of that one can be seen as part of today's Cross which stands in the Nethergate.

The Mercat Cross, 1586

Edward III pinches Dundee's Bells

In 1336, Edward I's grandson, Edward III of England, attacked Dundee and stole the town's bells. While they were at it, his soldiers thought it would be fun to fry a friar. So they got hold of a poor Dundee monk, burned him alive, then sailed off with the bells to Newcastle where they sold them.

By the middle of the 14th century, Dundee's trade in wool, wine and leather had picked up again. This was just as well because King David II of Scotland managed to get himself captured by

85

the English and Dundee had to foot some of the bill for the ransom to get him back.

Richard II's Burning Ambition

And in 1385 the English returned. The king on the English throne, Richard II, didn't bother with friars or church bells. King Richard just ordered his troops to kill as many Dundonians as they could find and (as usual) to burn the town to the ground.

87

medieval middens

Medieval houses had no toilets. Folk usually just made do with a bucket. When it was full, they tipped the bucket and its contents out into the street.

The Town Council did its best to keep the streets clean but there were that many steaming piles lying about, the street cleaners needed wheelbarrows to get it all up.

It became so bad that fines were dished out and people locked up in the Tolbooth on a charge of being a dirty midden. (As late as the 17th century, folk were still flinging their rubbish wherever they fancied.)

But it was hard work keeping clean in the Middle Ages. Folk couldn't just turn on a tap and wash their hands because they had no taps or running water in their houses. Rain or shine, Medieval Dundonians had to trudge down to one of the town's wells (like the Lady Well at the foot of the Hilltown) and bring back heavy buckets full of water.

Dundee Diary, 1400

Elizabeth Moncur, aged 9

I am tired today. Mother shouted at me this morning. She said I had to rise before the other girls. I go every day to draw water from the Lady Well. If I go slowly the Well will be busy. Mother says the water is clean but is soon made foul by the town girls laughing and gabbing and spilling their idle talk into the stream. I was up before the sun and brought the water home through the Dundee streets still shining with the frost.

My Father complains of his leg. It hurts, he says, when the snow is on the Corbie Hill. But he talks more of the English and their cannon that threw the ball from ships on the Tay that struck the roof in Tyndal's Wynd that fell down on Father's leg. That was in the years long past and I was not born. But still Father talks to me of the English and their cannon, as if I had seen the soldiers with my own eyes burn Dundee and break our houses with their guns.

I do not mind the English. They are far away. It is Father and his guns I do not like. He works in the forge with his Father and my uncles. I must bring them water to cool them in winter and in summer. I must watch the sparks do not jump to my frock or my hair. The men are silent at their labour, striking the metal with hammers. They do not see me. Only Uncle Andrew smiles. I hear them in the afternoons when they test a new gun on Mr Barrie's Meadow. I am pleased I am a girl and will not be a gun-maker's apprentice.

Mother says the Plague is in Edinburgh and will come to Dundee. Last year it visited Seagate. It stayed for a month with the Whittock people. The Plague took Thomas and Esme Whittock when it left, and twelve other bairns in Peter Street.

I pray to Saint Eloy in the town kirk for Esme's soul and for my friend, Anna. She is from the weavers that live on the Hill. Anna is sailed from Flanders a year past and does not talk like Dundee folk. Father tells me I should not speak over much with Anna. Her Father is not a Freeman like my Father. But I like her and we will watch the jugglers when the Lady Mary Fair comes, if there is no Plague in Dundee then.

It is for the Plague that Mother shouts at me to be quick with the water at the Well. I will be quick tomorrow and draw the water before the sun wakens the frost on the Murraygate stones.

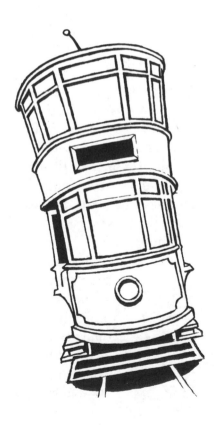

Dundee on the Move

For over a hundred years, no-one came and clobbered Dundee. Left in peace, the burgh grew in size.

With increased trade, the harbour became more important in the life of the town. As Dundee's merchants moved their shops and businesses to be nearer to it, the town centre shifted gradually from the once important Seagate to the Marketgate at the junction of the burgh's four main streets.

Handy for the harbour and the Murraygate, Seagate, Overgate and Nethergate, the Tolbooth and Town Cross were also flitted up to the Marketgate (now called the High Street), making it the hub of the busy burgh – as it is to this day.

Nobles and Neeps

Everyone knew their place in Medieval Dundee. At the top of the heap was the king. The **Constable** (usually a nobleman) was the king's man in Dundee. His job was to keep an eye on the burgesses on the Town Council. A burgess was a merchant or a townsperson with a bit of money in their pocket. The Town Council was in charge of more or less everything in the burgh and the head burgess was called the **Provost.** To make sure people did what he said, the Provost had a team of friendly **Bailies** to help him.

neeps

If you weren't one of these people, chances are you were at the bottom of the pile and probably spent much of your time pushing around cartloads of vegetables (or worse). You would be an Indweller, or to put it another way, a slave...

The Constable

The Provost

Bailies

...unless, that is, you managed to become a Freeman as a member of one of Dundee's **Trades**.

The Trades

The Dundee Trades have a long tradition and history in the city.

A Trade was made up of a group of craftsmen who did the same (or roughly the same) job. To keep standards high, a Master craftsman would take on a young apprentice to teach him the secrets of the trade. It could take up to four years to train a new apprentice and if the trainee mucked about during his apprenticeship, he would be bumped back down to the beginning and have to start all over again.

Apprentices had to pay to be trained but once they were accepted into a Trade, their name was written in a special ledger called a **Lockit Book**.

Only when your name was in the Lockit Book would you become a fully-fledged Freeman and be able to earn money within the burgh.

Craftsmen from outside the town who weren't members of a Dundee Trade did not get a very warm welcome.

95

The Nine Trades

The Maltmen, Wrights and Slaters stuck together as the Three Trades but most craftsmen belonged to one of the Nine Incorporated Trades.

**Baxters
(Bakers)**

**Cordiners
(Shoemakers)**

**Skinners
(Glovers)**

Tailors

Bonnetmakers

Fleshers
(Butchers)

Websters
(Weavers)

Hammermen
(Metal workers)

Litsters
(Dyers)

The Cannibal's Daughter

There is a story from the 15th century that on the outskirts of Dundee there lived a family who had a rather strange diet.

While some folk can happily tuck in to haggis and others enjoy getting their chompers into a big plate of stovies, the family in question had slightly different tastes to the rest of us – this lot liked to eat people.

Their weekly food shopping was done by ambushing lonely travellers and carrying them home to be served up as the evening meal. They even fed human flesh to their youngest child – a little baby girl.

The authorities were puzzled by these very mysterious disappearances and sent armed men to investigate. Before long the grisly (and probably quite gristly) truth was uncovered.

The cannibal, his wife and all their oldest children were put to death on the spot.

But the life of the infant girl was spared. She was taken to Dundee to be brought up in the care of a good family.

to be continued....

Punishment in Medieval Dundee

Breaking the law is never a good idea but in the Middle Ages in Dundee, it could be a particularly painful thing to do.

If you were caught pinching something, you could be pinned by your ear to the **Tron** (or weigh-beam) in the Marketgate.

nailed to the Tron for stealing

Gossips or folk who had a foul mouth could end up having to wear the **branks**.

The branks was a kind of helmet which had a vicious spike welded to it. When the helmet was fitted to your head, the spike went straight into your mouth, stopping you from swearing, gossiping, whistling, chewing gum ... doing anything really except breathing and wishing you'd kept your gub shut in the first place.

More Punishment

If you missed church even just once, you could be put in the **jougs**. This was an iron collar chained to the kirk door or Mercat Cross which the offender was then locked into by the neck.

Folk were often exiled for a few years or banished from the town forever.

And of course there was plenty of good old-fashioned hanging and burning.

The Cannibal's Daughter (continued)

As the lassie grew, folk noticed that she sometimes bit other children, then sucked the blood from the cut on their fingers.

It was feared that the girl was infected with cannibalism and that nothing could be done to help her. The law said that anyone who had a taste for human flesh had to suffer immediate execution.

But the girl was still a child. It was thought too cruel to harm someone as young as her.

So in their mercy, the authorities waited until the lass was eighteen years of age. And then they burned her alive in the Seagate.

Pirates on the Tay

One morning in 1490, the people of Dundee were awakened by the sound of cannons firing on the River Tay.

On the River Forth the day before, Stephen Bull, an English pirate, had ambushed the Scottish sea captain, Sir Andrew Wood, hoping to claim the bounty the King of England was offering for the Scotsman's head.

Sir Andrew, returning from Flanders with his two ships, the *Flower* and the *Yellow Carvel*, clashed with Bull's three ships within sight of Scotland. The fierce naval battle that followed lasted all that day and continued the next morning near Dundee at the mouth of the River Tay.

Sir Andrew Wood battling Captain Bull on the Tay

Thousands of locals crowded round the banks of the river to watch Sir Andrew defeat the pirates and lead the captured English ships into Dundee Harbour.

Hector Boece and the Hilltown

With so much history rattling about Dundee, it's no surprise that one of Scotland's most famous historians was a Dundonian.

Hector Boece (his name rhymes with Joyce) was born in 1465. He became a professor in Paris and helped found Aberdeen University.

Boece wrote in his book *Historia Gentis Scotorum* (History of the Scottish People) that Dundee folk were famous for the 'making of claith'. In other words, they were brilliant at weaving.

More brilliant weavers came to the town in the Middle Ages but the men of the Dundee Weavers Trade were a bit snotty about letting them in to work in the burgh.

So the new weavers set up their looms right at the edge of the burgh. The Hilltown, not officially part of Dundee until 1669, was settled by weavers from many different places. Its growing community became so famous for making cloth and bonnets, it was known for a long time simply as Bonnethill.

Many of the new weavers came from Flanders in Belgium

105

Dundee's Medieval Buildings

A large house called **Our Lady Warkstairs** once stood not far from the bus stops just outside Littlewoods.

Strathmartine's Lodging was built on ground now occupied by the City Square.

The town's **Weigh House** also stood on the site of the City Square.

Gardyne's Land on the High Street is Dundee's last surviving medieval merchant's house.

The Time Tram Guide to Dundee's Gates and Ports

Dundee's street names can be a little confusing but it's really dead easy to work out what they mean.

A **gate** is a road. You walk down or along a **gate**.

But a **Port** is actually a gate. You go through a **Port**.

Simple, eh? But just to keep you on your toes, **gate** is sometimes spelled **gait**.

Dundee once had seven Ports but only the Cowgate Port (or Wishart Arch) remains. Its six gates (or roads) are still there. The Overgate simply means the High Road and (surprise, surprise) the Nethergate is the Low Road. In the past, the Nethergate was known as the Flukergait (a fluker is a kind of fish). The Overgate had the name Argyllsgait after a man called Argyll and also because lots of Highlanders used to live there.

You can make the shape of Dundee just by lying down like this

The Old Steeple

- The Tower of St Mary's Church was completed in 1480.

- It's known locally as the Auld Steeple.

- 232 steps take you up to the top and back down again.

- Standing nearly 160 feet high, it is the oldest building in Dundee and is Scotland's largest medieval tower.

- From the cap-house on the roof, the town guard used to keep watch over the burgh.

- The English occupied the tower in 1548.

- After the church was destroyed during an attack on the town in 1645, the Tower stood on its own for 145 years.

- In 1651, it was the scene of Governor Lumsden's last stand against General Monck.

Walls, Wars and Witches

The Plague in Dundee

An outbreak of Plague in Medieval Dundee might have happened a bit like this:

- Ship from foreign port docks in Dundee harbour.
- Rats jump off ship.
- Tiny fleas carrying the virus jump off the rats.
- Flea bites Dundonian.
- Dundonian sneezes, coughs, turns purple then dies.
- Dead bodies start piling up in the street.

And before anyone could shout 'The Pest's in town', the Pest was in town. The Council ordered chains to be put across the harbour. Strangers approaching the West Port were in danger of getting shot at for fear they were bringing more Plague into the town.

111

The Sickmen's Yairds

Every time a dog comes into this country from abroad it has to stay locked up in special kennels in case it has any nasty diseases. That's what the Sickmen's Yairds were for – except they were for people.

With Dundee's streets and houses so close together, a virus could spread through it like wildfire. In 1349, the Plague almost wiped out the whole population and in 1607 an outbreak brought the town to a standstill for nearly two years. When it came to the Plague, the locals didn't take any chances.

So Dundee's sick and dying got carted off to big wooden sheds at the east end of the Seagate. Known as the Sickmen's Yairds, there the folk were left crammed together in the sweltering heat and freezing cold until they either a) got better or b) died.

In 1545 the Plague once again had Dundee in its grip. The preacher George Wishart is famous for climbing up on top of the Cowgate Port and praying for the terrified people inside the town and for the poor wretches lying out in the Sickmen's Yairds.

But George Wishart didn't really pray for anybody from the Cowgate Port. (He was dead long before the Port was even built.) But he did visit Dundee during the outbreak of Plague in 1545 to comfort the dying. The Port is called the Wishart Arch after him for his bravery and the kindness that he showed towards the people of Dundee.

The Wishart Arch (or Cowgate Port)

Dundee and the Reformation

The Scottish Reformation was a time of great change. During the Reformation, Scotland changed from being a (mostly) Catholic country to being a (mostly) Protestant one.

The Reformation started in Germany in 1517 when a monk called **Martin Luther** said he thought the Old Church had become too fancy. Religion, he said, should be more plain and simple.

So Martin did what a lot of folk do when they don't like something – he protested.

Dundee was a busy sea port with ships coming in all the time from France, Holland and Germany. Along with wine, salt and leather, the crews on these ships brought word of the new religion, Protestantism, which was sweeping Europe. The Protestant faith took hold in Dundee first before the rest of Scotland got to hear about it.

But like most major events in Scottish history, the Reformation didn't happen without a few things getting smashed up.

Protestant George Wishart was burnt at the stake in St Andrews in 1546 for his beliefs and in 1547 the people of Dundee began tearing down Devorguilla's ancient Monastery of the Greyfriars.

The Wedderburns

Three Dundee brothers who believed in the Reformation were John, James and Robert Wedderburn. But they didn't try to change things by smashing up churches or burning people. Instead, the Wedderburn boys used a pen – or in their case a big long feather with a splotch of ink on the end.

John Wedderburn took old poems which were a wee bit rude and wrote them out again, this time as polite religious verses. (His *Gude and Godlie Ballatis* are still in Dundee Central Library.)

His brother James wrote plays. In 1540 James' drama *The Beheading of Johne the Baptist* was performed in the open air in Dundee.

And Robert is said to have been the author of a big book entitled *The Complaynt of Scotland*.

115

Dundee and the Rough Wooing

Around the same time, Henry VIII of England (without even asking if they fancied each other) proposed a wedding between his son, Edward, and the young Mary Queen of Scots. The Scottish lords told Henry to shove it but the English king would not take no for an answer.

He sent his army north and burned Edinburgh to the ground. His plan, nicknamed the 'Rough Wooing', was to bang the Scots' heads together until they agreed to the marriage. The plan didn't work because Mary married the future king of France instead. But even though Henry VIII died, there was still more trouble in store for the ordinary Scottish people.

In September 1547, the Scots were defeated by the English at the Battle of Pinkie near Edinburgh and that same month, English soldiers stormed Broughty Castle. From there a few months later in early 1548, they mounted an invasion of Dundee.

There wasn't much the Scots could do to stop them. Most Dundee men were in their beds recovering from the Plague of 1545 and the Scottish army was still seeing stars after the Battle of Pinkie. When the English invaded Dundee, their soldiers simply walked in without a shot being fired.

Invasion of Dundee, 1548

The English were only in Dundee for a short time when they heard that a large force of French soldiers were on their way to rescue the town. Before escaping, the English filled their pockets with goodies and set fire to the buildings. As usual, St Mary's Church was the first thing to get done over. Its altars were stripped of gold and the walls knocked down. The English even helped themselves to the kirk bells again.

When the French soldiers arrived, they tried to put out the flames but it was too late for St Mary's which had already burned to the ground.

117

The Siege of Broughty Castle

The English retreated to Broughty Castle a few miles from Dundee. From there they made a right nuisance of themselves. They rode around like mad on horseback terrorising the locals and fired cannons at ships travelling up and down the Tay. They even built a second stronghold on Forthill at Balgillo.

The Scots and the French tried to push the English out of Broughty Castle but they couldn't shift them. The English garrison managed to hold out for three years before finally leaving in 1550.

The French in Dundee

During that time, the French were in control of Dundee. In the beginning, the Dundee folk hailed the French soldiers as heroes for chasing the English out of their town. But as the years went on, the people started to get a bit fed up of them.

In 1552, Alexander Paterson complained to the burgh court that some French soldiers had been pinching cabbages out of his garden.

A Walled Town At Last

Whenever Edinburgh or Stirling came under attack during the Middle Ages, its citizens could hide behind their town's massive thick stone walls. Dundonians, however didn't have this luxury because their town didn't have any walls at all. Instead whenever the enemy showed up outside Dundee, the Town Council hurried through the streets shouting at folk to close the gates at the bottom of their back gardens.

119

But by the 1590s a wall had been put up to protect the town. It ran round the centre of old Dundee (following roughly the same route as today's ring road). People entered and left through the town's Ports.

Usually locked at night, the Ports were open during the day but could be closed quickly to stop an unfriendly army marching in or to keep out a dose of the deadly Plague.

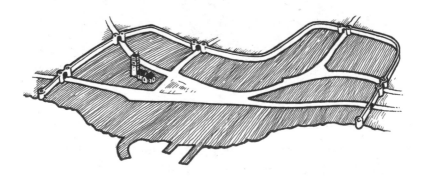

The Howff

(The Dead Centre of Dundee)

Until the reign of Mary Queen of Scots, dead Dundonians were buried in the graveyard of St Clement's Church. This ancient kirk stood on ground between the Marketgate and the harbour (where the modern City Square is today).

Under the city square?

Mary Queen of Scots, visiting Dundee in 1564, was shocked to see the market traders selling meat and milk so close to the town graveyard.

The Monastery of the Greyfriars had been destroyed in the Reformation and its orchard was lying empty. Mary granted the land to the town so it could be used as a new burial ground.

the howff

A Howff Who's Who

Dundee's Howff cemetery is full of interesting headstones, beautifully carved symbols and, of course, lots and lots of dead people.

Over 1,400 gravestones mark the final resting place of thousands of Dundee's former citizens. James Chalmers, inventor, and John Glas, founder of the Glassite Church in King Street, have monuments above their graves while other stones bear simple inscriptions for ordinary folk with good Dundee names like Cox, Low, Robertson and Fleming.

weavers' symbol

mariner's headstone

But the fascinating thing about the Howff is the fancy carving which appears on many of the headstones. It's possible to work out which job a person did during their life just by looking at the unusual markings.

angels show where young children lie

A grave showing pictures of leopards with a shuttle in their mouths means it belongs to a weaver. The sign of a ship's wheel tells you that a sailor or a sea captain lies down below. And angels mark the graves of young children.

The Meeting Stone

Graveyards can be spooky places but the men of the Trades in Dundee didn't let that sort of thing bother them. The likes of the Butchers, Bakers and Bonnetmakers would have their meetings outside in the open air around the grave of one of their former masters. And when the Trades wanted to have a blether all together, they gathered around the special Meeting Stone.

David Wedderburn's Compt Book

Throughout its history, the harbour has always been the key to Dundee's success.

If the harbour was busy, the town was doing well and folk had silver in their pockets. But if the harbour was damaged in a storm or its ships stolen by a foreign army or shut because of Plague, then the town lost out and times for the people were hard.

Times were good though when David Wedderburn was writing his *Compt Book*. A descendant of the Wedderburn writers, David's journal gives a clear picture of the goods coming in to and going out from Dundee at the turn of the 17th century.

Dundee and the National Covenant

In 1587, Mary Queen of Scots had her head cut off by her cousin, Queen Elizabeth I of England, but in 1603, Mary's son, King James VI of Scotland, was crowned King James I of England after Queen Elizabeth died without an heir.

King James VI <u>and</u> I

Some Scots grumbled about having to share their king with the English but the fireworks really started when James' son, King Charles I, wanted to make the Scottish church more like the English one.

When Charles told the Scots they had to use an English prayer book in church, people from all over Scotland (including Dundee) signed a very important paper called the **National Covenant**.

The Covenant said that Christ was more important than the king and not the other way around, but some Scots remained loyal to Charles.

One Scotsman who was at first against him only to become his most constant supporter was James Graham, the Marquis of Montrose. A brilliant military leader, he took a bunch of Irish and Scottish troops on a tour of Scotland duffing up anyone they met who was in favour of the Covenant.

Dundee folk however were strongly in favour of the Covenant. In fact, they thought the Covenant was great. It wasn't long before the Marquis paid the town a visit.

Montrose Batters Dundee

On 4th of April 1645 with a force of 750 men, Montrose called upon the town to surrender or else. When the Dundonians told him to buzz off, Montrose attacked.

Although Dundee's thick walls could have kept him out for days, there was one weak spot beside the Corbie Hill. The town had all its heavy guns up on this hill but the wall around it was needing repaired. Montrose sent his Irish troops to storm that part of the wall. They quickly broke through it and let the rest of Montrose's soldiers (fierce clansmen from the Scottish Highlands) into the town.

The invaders also captured Corbie Hill (which is where Lindsay Street is today) and turned Dundee's guns round so

they were facing their own town. Then, standing calmly by, Montrose ordered his men to open fire.

Montrose's troops blasted, burned, burgled and bullied Dundee for several hours before a large Covenanter army was

spotted approaching the town. Montrose led his men out of Dundee just in the nick of time.

St Mary's Church was badly damaged in the attack. As a result, the Old Steeple stood all on its own for the next 145 years.

Oliver Cromwell in Scotland

By 1649, another royal head was on the chopping block. In January that year the English Parliament executed King Charles I.

Although they'd recently been fighting against him, the Scots were outraged. Charles was their king too and there was the English Parliament rudely slicing their monarch's napper off without even asking them.

Charles I
1600–1649

So the Scots invited Charles' son (also called Charles) to be their new king and crowned him Charles II at Scone near Perth on New Year's Day, 1651.

The English Parliament at that time didn't believe in monarchs. They'd already got rid of one and they certainly didn't need any more popping up. Even before Charles was crowned, the English army was in Scotland trying to make the Scots forget about daft things like kings.

The English soldiers had the nickname 'Roundheads' because they wore round helmets. The chief Roundhead was Oliver Cromwell.

By the summer of 1651, the English controlled most of Scotland. Cromwell had beaten the Scots army at Dunbar, elbowed them in the guts at Edinburgh and skelped their backsides at Stirling. But one Scottish town had so far escaped a thumping. Dundee remained fiercely loyal to Charles. (They had even had him over to tea a couple of times.) Cromwell wasn't about to let Dundee off the hook.

And, as an added incentive, there was a lot of loot in the town just waiting to be pinched. The place was quite literally 'minted'.

Oliver Cromwell
1599–1658

Cromwell's Roundheads burning a Scottish village

For months, the Scots lords and merchants had been whisking their valuables off to the burgh on the north shore of the River Tay. Thinking their gold and silver and sparkly necklaces would be safe behind the town's thick walls, the Scots even moved the Mint (which made all of Scotland's money) from Edinburgh to Dundee.

In July 1651, Dundee was full of rebels and dosh but it was also bristling with guns manned by proud Dundonians ready to die for their town.

131

Cromwell (who had to return to England to fight Charles II at Worcester) knew he couldn't pick just any old soldier to deal with Dundee.

So he sent the toughest, meanest old soldier in his army. Cromwell sent General Monck.

Born in Devon in 1608, George Monck rose to become a trusted soldier and general in several English armies.

He fought at home and abroad for Charles I...then he switched sides and served in Oliver Cromwell's army... before switching back to put Charles II back on the throne.

George Monck
1608–1670

He died in 1670 after a military career that took him to Ireland, Spain, Holland – and Dundee.

The Siege of Dundee, 1651

By the summer of that year, the people of Dundee were already busy preparing for a visit from the English Roundhead army.

The town wall was hastily repaired and strengthened. Houses standing just outside the wall were knocked down so that enemy riflemen wouldn't be able to hide behind them. The town was split into four fighting units – Nethergate, Overgate, Murraygate and Seagate – with captains put in charge of each quarter. The guns on the town wall were given a good polish and some of them were aimed out at the River Tay in case of an attack by sea.

By August, the Dundonians were ready for anything the English could throw at them, which was just as well because it wasn't long before the English started throwing it.

They pelted Dundee with cannon fire from the land and blasted it from gunboats out on the river but the town walls held firm.

On the 26th of August, General Monck ordered Dundee's Governor, Sir Robert Lumsden, to surrender. Governor Lumsden told Monck to get lost.

Lumsden refusing to surrender to General Monck

The Dundonians' spirits were high. They had plenty food and supplies to keep them going and, best of all, there was a big thick wall between them and the English. The townsfolk were optimistic they could hold out until Scottish reinforcements arrived.

But their hopes of a rescue were dashed when General Monck's men arrested the leaders of the Scottish government's army near Dundee and locked them up in Broughty Ferry Castle.

And then a young Scottish boy unwittingly told the English that Dundee's soldiers liked to have a drink and bit of a long lie in the morning. With this knowledge, Monck led a full-scale assault of the town at dawn on the 1st of September.

Dundee Diary, August 1651

My Father and Halyburton's son, they call me bairn, so I climb the Wall and I talk with the English like a man.

When it is dawn and the Dundee guards leave their watch and go to the taverns for their meat, I pass the guns on Corbie Hill. I climb the Dundee Wall and go out into the camps to the English Roundheads.

They warn me not to play near the Wall but they care only about the silver which came in carts from Edinburgh and Perth during the summer. When one of the Overgate sergeants stopped me, he said if he caught me by my lugs again I would soon lie in the Howff among my grandfathers.

Halyburton's son will not come with me. He says the English will kill me and kill him too. My hands are scratched from the climbing. Dundee's Wall is old and the holds are sore to find. But I have been in their camps and still I live.

The English are in the Playfield and on Scrymgeour's land. They are everywhere. They are strange and have round hats. Everyone calls them Roundheads and spits. I hear their guns all day but still they do not break the Wall. We hear them call to us to surrender but Sir Robert Lumsden says we must be strong and defeat them.

Halyburton's son knows I cross the Wall but I have not told him I speak with the English. I tell them nothing of our guns or of the gold hidden in the houses and the ships in the harbour filled with treasure.

The English ask about our men and when they sleep. I tell them they never sleep, that they are always on watch. They like me to talk about our men and their breakfast. I say they breakfast as always, which is the truth. The Dundee soldiers take eggs and meat and bread and wash it down with beer. Sometimes they drink a lot of beer and sleep a little but they never leave their guns.

The English are strange. They stopped their talking after I told them about our men and how they had their breakfast. They ordered me to go home to my mother. I will climb the Wall back into Dundee and speak with them no more.

The Massacre of Dundee

Monck's men won control of the town. In those days it was traditional for a victorious army to be allowed one day (and one day only) to rough the locals up a bit, steal whatever they could find, eat the town's supply of sweets and burn the odd house and church to the ground.

But Monck's men didn't stop after one day. Monck was angry at the Dundonians for not surrendering sooner so he let his troops do what they wanted for as long as they wanted.

Monck's soldiers killed over a thousand men, women and children in Dundee. The slaughter only stopped when a baby was seen crying next to its dead mother, a sight which moved even the cruel Roundheads to pity.

The Siege of the Old Steeple

When Monck's soldiers broke through the wall and swarmed into town, Sir Robert Lumsden and a handful of brave Scotsmen retreated to the tower of St Mary's and began shooting at the English soldiers in the streets below. Monck surrounded the tower and returned fire.

With bullets whizzing around their heads and with zero chance of escape, the Scots held the Old Steeple for three days. On the third day, the attackers set fire to bales of damp straw at the foot of the tower in a bid to smoke the defenders out.

Coughing and choking, the Dundee men emerged and surrendered to General Monck. But the general, furious that

Lumsden had not surrendered the first time round, ordered all of them beheaded.

Governor Lumsden's head was stuck on a spike halfway up the tower he had so bravely defended. It hung there for nine years before it eventually fell off and clattered to the ground.

Sir Robert Lumsden's heid, 1651–1660

Monck's Tower

The English army remained in Dundee for several years and Cromwell made General Monck the Governor of Scotland.

His headquarters in Dundee were in a house at the entrance to the old Overgate.

The house known as Monck's Tower was still standing in the 1960s.

It was knocked down to make way for the Overgate Centre.

Gold in the Tay

Once Monck's men had finished doing in the townsfolk, they started on the town itself.

The English pulled down the city walls that had held them out. Then they helped themselves to the Scottish gold and silver the Scottish toffs had hidden in the town. Piling the whole lot into sixty Scottish ships stolen from Dundee harbour, they sailed out onto the Tay homeward bound for England.

But within sight of the town and in good weather, the ships mysteriously sank. All hands were lost and the treasure was never recovered. Some say the gold, worth £2 billion in today's money, is still down there beneath the waves in the shifting sands of the Tay riverbed.

Grissel Jaffray

When Monck's army left, the people of Dundee were safe once more to walk the streets of their own home town. But for inhabitants like Grissel Jaffray, Dundee was still full of danger.

Probably for no better reason than one of her neighbours just didn't like her very much, Grissel Jaffray was accused of being a 'witch'. Anyone found guilty of witchcraft was usually hanged and then burned at the stake.

ABOOT 2500 FOLK WERE KILLT FOR WITCHCRAFT IN SCOTLAND

kens aathin

Scotland was not a healthy place to be if someone called you a witch. One of the busiest times for the hangman was during the reign of Charles II. An irrational fear of witches gripped the land and Grissel, an old woman by then, was thrown in the Dundee Tolbooth on suspicion of being in league with the devil.

The Dundee magistrates found her guilty and sentenced her to be put to death.

BURN HER ALEHVE!

HAVERS ALERT!

There is a legend that tells of Grissel Jaffray's son who was a sailor returning home to Dundee from a long sea journey. As his ship landed, he asked about the smoke rising from the Seagate. A witch was that day being burnt for her crimes. When the sailor asked who the witch was, he was told his own mother's name. The story goes that he walked back to the shore, got aboard another ship and sailed away from Dundee, never to return.

Grissel Jaffray was burnt at the stake in the Seagate on 23rd of November 1669. Although this cruel practice continued until well into the next century, she was the last person to be executed for witchcraft in Dundee.

Bonnie Dundee

In 1689, the peace of Dundee was threatened once again, this time by a man who was actually called 'Dundee'.

In fact, he had quite a few names. He was born John Graham of Claverhouse but he was later given the nickname 'Bloody Clavers' because as a soldier in the service of the king he spilled a lot of blood chasing Covenanters around the south of Scotland.

Claypotts Castle

The king who also had two names (James VII of Scotland and James II of England) rewarded Claverhouse for his services to blood-spilling with the title 'Viscount Dundee'. The new Viscount was a handsome man and so he ended up with another nickname for his collection, 'Bonnie Dundee.'

Not only was he the bonniest man in Dundee, he was one of the richest too with a choice of three castles to live in – Dudhope, Mains o Claverhouse and Claypotts Castle near Douglas.

The First Jacobite Rebellion, 1689

The town of Dundee didn't have much to do with the first Jacobite rebellion but John Graham of Claverhouse certainly did.

In 1688 his pal, James VII, was kicked out of his job as king. Claverhouse wanted to put poor James back on the throne. The very next year he raised the royal flag on Dundee Law and charged off to fight.

He won a famous victory against the government's troops at

Killiecrankie near Pitlochry in July 1689 but Claverhouse managed to get shot during the battle and died shortly after from his wounds.

Bonnie Dundee flew the royal standard on the Law on 4th April 1689. Four months later, he was dead.

But years after his death, Scotland's top poets were still writing about this man who in life was both 'bloody' and 'bonnie'.

Bonnie Dundee

Robert Burns wrote a famous song about the battle of Killiecrankie and Sir Walter Scott composed 'The Bonnets of Bonnie Dundee' which is one of Scotland's best known songs.

Come fill up my cup, come fill up my can,
Come saddle my horses and call out my men,
Unhook the West Port, and let us go free,
For it's up wi the bonnets o Bonnie Dundee.

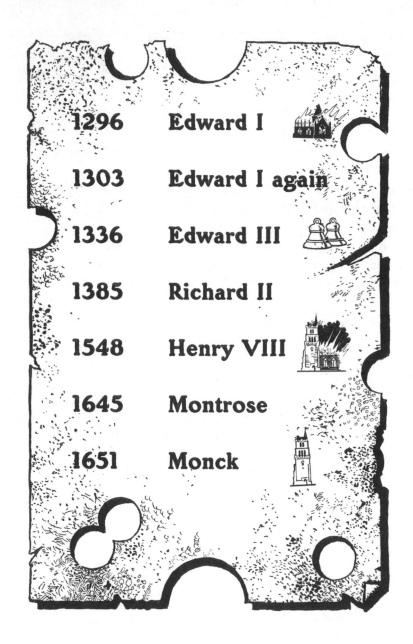

1296	Edward I
1303	Edward I again
1336	Edward III
1385	Richard II
1548	Henry VIII
1645	Montrose
1651	Monck

Oranges and Linen

Not So Bonnie Dundee

At the end of the 17th century, Dundee was not the bonnie place it had once been.

Dundee harbour in 1668

Monck's soldiers left behind a community of old men, widows and orphans. Dundee's grand medieval churches and mansions lay in ruins. And the burgh didn't have a penny to its name.

As if that wasn't enough, the Dundee folk had to deal with a run of very bad luck before the century was brought coughing and spluttering to a close.

A freak storm in 1658 destroyed the town harbour. Ten years later in 1668, a second wild storm smashed it up again. Dundonians went hungry from 1685 when severe frosts, drought and rain ruined seven harvests in a row. And in 1694, the Plague returned to plague Dundee's bruised and battered citizens.

The Dundee Elephant

But if the people were having a hard time of it, spare a thought for the poor elephant which keeled over and died on the road to Broughty Ferry in 1706.

Patrick Blair, a Dundee surgeon, was a keen botanist who normally only got to study insects, flowers and small animals. But when the news came that a whole elephant from a travelling circus had expired on a nearby road, he immediately grabbed his medical bag and ran out with a large saw to dissect the exotic creature. (In other words, he wanted to cut the big beastie open and have a look inside.)

For three days, a large crowd oohed and aahed and tried not

to pass out as they watched the doctor hack away at the huge creature.

Patrick Blair's claim to fame is that he was the first person in the world to perform a dissection on an elephant. And when he wasn't sawing up elephants, Blair, in his spare time, was a Jacobite.

The Old and Young Pretenders

Like Bonnie Dundee in 1689, the Jacobites wanted a king from the Stuart family to be on the throne. In 1715 someone else was sitting on it so Blair swapped his scalpel for a sword and set off to fight for a man called James Stuart. His other name was the Old Pretender. He spent one night in Dundee's Seagate during the second Jacobite rising but the Dundonians weren't too keen to risk their necks for him. The Old Pretender didn't become king and Patrick Blair got a short spell in prison for his trouble.

In 1745, another man from the Stuart family who tried to become king (and didn't) was Bonnie Prince Charlie. Dundonians showed more enthusiasm for this third Jacobite rising, a lot of them following Charlie on an invasion of England before ending up in a bloody grave at the Battle of Culloden near Inverness in 1746.

The Success of Linen

How Dundee Turned This into This

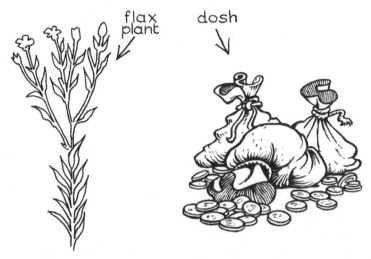

flax plant

dosh

Dundee's weavers had been spinning and weaving the flax that grew in the fields around the town for centuries.

From flax you can weave linen and in the 18th century the demand for Dundee linen became so great that extra flax had to be brought in from Russia. New mills powered by water brought people in from the countryside to work and Dundee grew rapidly into one of the biggest producers of linen in the country.

Dundee's trade may have been on the up but its buildings still looked like they had been in the wars (which of course they had). The town centre boasted a ruined church, an abandoned graveyard and a shabby old tolbooth.

In 1731, the town got back some of its former glory with a new town house designed by the famous architect, William Adam. Nicknamed 'The Pillars', the Town House was dear to the hearts of Dundee's people.

Dundee's grand Town House, 1731–1931

For two hundred years, folk met under its arches to buy and sell goods and to catch up on the latest gossip. It was a sad day for Dundee when it was knocked down in 1931 to make way for the new City Square.

One place where there was real room for improvement was at the east end of the Marketgate. There stood the town's Shambles (or slaughter house) where pigs, cows and sheep had been getting the chop since the Middle Ages.

In the year 1776 the Nine Incorporated Trades who had been meeting by a stone in the Howff graveyard built themselves a brand new meeting place.

The elegant Trades Hall was built by Samuel Bell on the site of the dirty old Shambles.

Bell also built St Andrews Church beside the Wellgate which is the spiritual home of the Dundee Trades. (Bell Street is named after him.)

Dundee's Trades Hall stood for a hundred years before it was demolished to let trams in and out of the Murraygate.

Admiral Duncan

Born in 1731 in the Seagate, Adam Duncan was brought up among the sights and sounds of Dundee harbour. He joined the British navy as a young man and rose through the ranks to become an Admiral of the Fleet.

**Adam Duncan
1731–1804**

In 1797, Great Britain was at war with France. Holland, France's ally, was getting ready to invade England and Admiral Duncan had orders to stop them. On 11th of October, off the Holland coast near a place called Camperdown, in heavy fog, Duncan bravely sailed his ships through the middle of the Dutch fleet and then blasted them right out of the water.

The Battle of Camperdown, 1797

On his return, Duncan was greeted as a national hero. There is a large mansion house on the outskirts of Dundee named Camperdown after his famous naval victory, built by his son.

American 'Spies'

Around 1800, the people were terrified that the French were about to invade the shores of Great Britain at any minute. At Hartlepool in the north of England, there is a story that the fisher folk there were so twitchy that they hanged a ship's monkey thinking he was a French spy.

The Hartlepool monkey

At Dundee in 1801, it wasn't a monkey that confused the locals but two young American students. John Bristed and Andrew Cowan had taken a break from their studies at Edinburgh University and crossed the River Forth into Fife. To make their trip more fun they thought it would be a good laugh to dress in strange clothes and speak in Latin.

By the time they reached Dundee, the locals had decided that they were dangerous French spies and should be executed (remember the monkey?). Only when a friend from Edinburgh explained who they really were did the Dundee folk see the funny side. Early next morning, just in case, the two students skipped breakfast and got out of Dundee as fast as they could.

Keiller's Marmalade

At the end of the 18th century, it's possible that a ship from Spain got caught in a North Sea storm and turned in to Dundee harbour for shelter.

At the dockside, maybe a Dundonian sweet-maker called John Keiller got talking to the Spanish captain who told him he had some boxes of Seville oranges in the hold. Oranges were rare in Dundee in those days so who's to say John Keiller didn't buy the lot and take them home to his wife, Janet, in their sweet-maker's shop to see if she could do anything with them. No-one knows if this story is true or not but when their son, James, and his wife, Margaret, took over the family business, Keiller's Marmalade became a household name.

To people at that time, marmalade was an exotic treat and it was often served up as a dessert on special occasions. The Dundee folk certainly had a sweet tooth and generations of them munched their way through thousands of jars of the stuff, helping to make the Keiller's brand a worldwide success.

Rights and Riots

In the early 1800s, ordinary people didn't have many rights. If they spoke up about something they didn't like, they could easily find themselves in jail or even transported to prison colonies in Australia. Only rich men were free to speak their minds and vote in elections.

But around the world ordinary folk were giving their so-called masters a good hard kick in the pants. When the people in Dundee heard about the revolutions in America and France, they wanted to know why they didn't have the same rights as the rich.

Dundee's many weavers were a well-read lot and a book called *The Rights of Man* by Thomas Paine made many question the authority of the Provost and the Town Council to tell them what to do.

George Mealmaker was a weaver who did more than just read books. He formed an organisation called the United Scotsmen to challenge the ruling classes. But Mealmaker was a troublemaker in the eyes of the law and he was sent to Australia where he died.

George Mealmaker
1768–1808

Frances Wright
1795–1853

Born in Dundee's Nethergate, **Frances Wright** used words to fight injustice. She became famous at home and in the United States for writing books and making speeches. Arguing that everyone should have the right to vote, Frances also worked her whole life to bring an end to slavery.

But the fight for equal rights was not always about books. There was often shouting, bawling and the occasional riot on the streets of Dundee.

157

The Tree of Liberty

The Provost who had the tough job of controlling Dundee's citizens during those turbulent times was Andrew Riddoch.

A colourful character himself, Riddoch managed to hold on to the top job of Provost for about forty years. His mansion still stands in the Nethergate.

Planting a Liberty Tree in the middle of town was something Americans did to celebrate their freedom. Not to be outdone, a group of reformers decided that Dundee High Street should have a Liberty Tree too. So late one night in 1793 they pinched a young sapling out of someone's garden and planted it beside the Mercat Cross.

Provost Riddoch, woken by the noise, came out in his night gown to see what all the racket was about. The protesters couldn't believe their luck. They made the Provost run three times round the tree in his jammies shouting, 'Liberty and Equality for Ever.'

Provost Riddoch dancing round the Liberty Tree

But Riddoch had his revenge though. Flanked by heavily armed soldiers, he returned to the tree the very next day and had it dug up.

George Kinloch

Dundonian George Kinloch kept up the fight for freedom by making political speeches about reform. The authorities, however, thought he had a big mouth. After a powerful speech to 6,000 people in Dundee, George had to escape to France to avoid being arrested.

But in 1832 the Reform Act was passed, allowing George Kinloch to return home where he stood for election and won. Sadly, he was to die just one year after becoming Dundee's first Member of Parliament.

George Kinloch
1775–1833

The 1832 Reform Act gave more people than ever before (but not everyone) the right to vote. The Dundee folk were chuffed to bits. The Council marked the occasion by blowing up the hill which used to stand between the High Street and Meadowside. And then they built a new road in its place and called it Reform Street.

And in a second less official celebration, the locals showed their delight by pulling a boat out of the harbour. They then set it on fire and dragged it joyfully through the streets for a couple of days.

Other people chose to welcome in the new age by going for a ride on the Dundee to Newtyle Railway, which was opened in 1831.

This was no ordinary railway. To travel from Dundee to the village of Newtyle north of the town, the train and its carriages had to pass through a 500 foot long tunnel blasted right through the Dundee Law.

The Law railway tunnel opened in 1831

Mill-girls and Millionaires

Victorian Dundee

A Whale of a Time

Dundonians had been netting fish for their tea for centuries but in 1753 they went hunting for something a little bigger.

Dundee's first whaling ship, the *Dundee*, sailed to Greenland that year, caught four whales, chopped them up, sailed home and sold their oil and meat. More ships, with exotic names like the *Calypso*, the *Polynia*, and the *Terra Nova*, were soon leaving each spring to grab a share of the valuable whales swimming about in the freezing cold waters of the Davis Straits.

When they couldn't get hold of whales, they went after seals. In 1866 alone, just four Dundee whaling ships came home laden down with the skins of 58,000 seals between them.

But whaling was dangerous for the whalers too. Each ship had to sail through fields of floating ice and if one got trapped in the floes, that was usually the end of it. The ice simply crushed it to pieces. In all, forty Dundee ships were lost on the icy seas.

Thar She Blows!

In the northern waters, when a whale was sighted, small boats were lowered from the main ship and the whalers rowed out to catch their prey.

Dundee whalers harpooning a humpback whale off Greenland

Four Ways to Die on a Whaling Trip

Whaling was definitely not a healthy occupation. Any number of horrible things could happen to a person on a whaling ship and, so you don't have too many nightmares, here are just four of them:

1. Drowning
Not surprisingly, the whales didn't take too kindly to being jagged in the backside with six foot long harpoons. An angry whale could easily capsize the tiny whaling boat, flipping the whole crew over into the icy waves.

2. Frostbite
The bitterly cold air gave the crewmen frostbite which freezes the blood and can make fingers and toes drop off. (Some whalers were that tough they kept their frostbitten thumbs and big toes in their pockets to show the folks back home.)

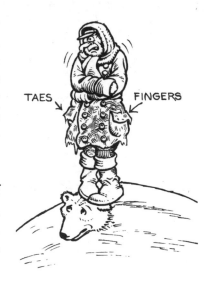

TAES   FINGERS

3. Scurvy
Scurvy, a disease you can get if you don't eat any fresh fruit and vegetables for a few months, made the whalers' gums go black and their teeth fall out.

4. Bears
Sometimes the whalers were marooned on the ice and got chased around by hungry polar bears.

Toshie

In 1867, harpooner James McIntosh (nicknamed Toshie) was in a whaling boat that drifted away from its mother ship, the *Chieftain*, in a thick fog. The crew of five tried to row to Iceland in the tiny whaling boat. They were at sea in freezing temperatures for sixteen days before they were finally rescued.

Everyone was dead except Toshie, who was in a pretty bad way himself. He had frostbite in both legs which had to be amputated.

But Toshie wasn't beaten. Fitted with a new pair of wooden legs, he cycled to London to campaign for the rights of disabled sailors.

Top Port

By the middle of the 19th century, Dundee was Britain's top whaling port. In faster stronger ships powered by steam, the Dundee fleet doubled in size and over the next half century it went out and pulverised thousands more whales.

It is now against the law to hunt whales which is just as well because the whaling industry in the 19th and 20th centuries killed off nearly all of them. Dundee stopped whaling in 1918. Its last ship was the *Balaena*.

The whaling ships are gone and the whalers all dead but Mary Ann Lane (named for a ship that sank off Canada), Candle Lane and Whale Lane are reminders of a time when Dundee men risked their lives and chased mighty whales through the icy northern seas.

Stinking Rich

There was good money in a dead whale. Its oil fuelled the town's street lamps. The candles which lit Dundee's homes were made from whale tallow (or fat). Whalebone was jammed into fashionable ladies' corsets so they could look thinner without holding their stomachs in.

But boiling up the whales' bodies to produce all these things was a foul business. Dundee folk grumbled constantly about the evil smells which wafted across town from the boiling yards at the docks.

Stowaways

When a whaler was about to set sail, its crew would have a quick hunt round for young lads trying to stow away on the ship. Hauled by the ears out of barrels or dragged out from under piles of sacks, the lads were sent back to shore with a boot in the backside ... only to be back the next day trying to hide on board another ship.

The thought of scurvy, death and ending up with a wooden leg didn't seem to bother them. Sailing on a whaling ship had to be more exciting than life in one of Dundee's gloomy mills.

Some lads were slippery enough to avoid capture until the ship was well out to sea. The captain had no choice but to take them on as crew members to work as deck hands or cabin boys for the rest of the trip.

Cox's Stack

At 280 feet high, Cox's Stack towers above the city's skyline, a reminder of the days when Dundee was the world capital of jute.

It was built in 1865 by Cox Brothers for their new jute mill in Lochee. With over 100 other mills in the town, they wanted their chimney to be the tallest and best in Dundee. Splashing out £6,000 (a huge sum at that time), they ordered it built to a swish Italian design.

The jute mill that was to stand next to such a posh lum would have to be an extra special one – and it was.

Camperdown Works in the 1860s employed 5,000 workers, making it one of the largest factories in Europe. It even had its own railway station. It was so big that the tiny village of Lochee next door quickly tripled in size as workers came to toil in the shadow of Cox's Stack.

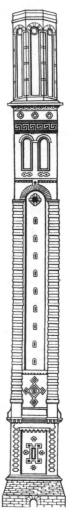

Jute and Dundee

Jute is cheap, strong and can be made into just about anything. In the early 19th century, the world was going crazy for it.

The jute plant grows naturally in warm countries like India and Bangladesh, and the lush Subcontinent is the best place to spin and weave its fibres. The Indians and Bangladeshis, however, had no big mills to mass produce jute and no modern harbours to ship it out. But (although it was on the other side of the planet) Dundee had both.

The town, by 1825, had a new dock for its busy harbour (built by the famous engineer, Thomas Telford) and a skilled workforce used to banging out millions of yards of linen. Switching from weaving flax to weaving jute wasn't a problem. The snag was the Dundee weather: it was rubbish.

Well, not rubbish exactly, but much colder than in India. When it was first brought to Dundee, the jute didn't like the Scottish climate. Every time someone had a go at spinning jute, the thread just snapped. Although it was much cheaper, Dundee's mills ignored this awkward new fibre and carried on making linen from flax.

Then one day some clever clogs knocked a bucket of whale oil over a batch of jute by mistake. It was discovered that the whale oil made the jute fibre soft and stopped it from breaking. As luck would have it, Dundee just happened to be the top whaling port in the whole of Great Britain. Getting a good supply of whale oil would not be hard to arrange. By the 1830s, the scene was set for Dundee to begin its wild adventure with jute.

A Woman's Town

Keeping a big heavy handloom going all day takes a lot of effort. Although many women could have easily handled the job, in the early 19th century weaving in Dundee was done mostly by men. Women merely helped out, spinning thread for the men to weave.

The invention of the power loom, however, soon changed all that. To operate a power loom, all a person needs is a bit of common sense and nimble hands. Strength has nothing to do with it.

Always looking to save money, the mill owners started to employ more and more women. They were just as good at weaving as the men and in those days the bosses didn't have to pay women a full wage.

By the 1850s, eight out of ten women in Dundee worked in the jute industry while many husbands helped out in the mills or stayed at home to look after the bairns.

1. Flax weaver 2. Flax spinner 3. Jute weaver 4. Kettle biler

Jute's Journey Around the World

The jute started out in India where it was harvested. Fast clipper ships brought it to Dundee. There it was spun and woven into rough cloth.

That cloth was then turned into sacks for carrying coal around the country, sandbags for soldiers to hide behind so they wouldn't get shot and sails for ships on the high seas. Armies slept in tents made of Dundee jute and the settlers making their way through the American West travelled in wagons covered with the stuff.

Dundee Diary, Annie McDonald
September 1863

Mr Baxter has made a park. Today the spinners and weavers of Dundee had the day away from the mill to help Mr Baxter open his new park. They say sixty thousand Dundee folk were on the field at Arbroath Road with its lawns and flower beds and pavilion bigger than a house.

About a hundred people stay in our house. We live in Sugarhouse Wynd by Seagate. Father loads cargo at the docks and Mother is full time at Upper Dens Mill. John, my brother, is aboard a whaler. Mother begged him not to go on the oily smelly ship but he said he did not want to work at the weaving. He always called me 'mill-girl' and laughed.

But I am not a mill-girl. I am a part-timer at Gilroy's Mill. I go to the small schoolroom they have there. It is always full of children half asleep or coughing from the mill dust. I listen to the teacher tell us about counting and grammar. He shows us on the map places like Russia and the Argentine before we go back to our work in the mill.

I am writing this so I remember the fine day at Mr Baxter's new park. I will go there again soon after my classes. It was a grand sight all those people together in the sun, but tomorrow I must go to the mill.

Millionaires

Jute brought great wealth to the mill owners of Dundee.

With their immense fortunes, they built themselves palaces on the outskirts of the town like Carbet Castle in Broughty Ferry (above).

However, instead of putting their money back into Dundee, they bought enormous Texan cattle ranches and invested in American railways.

In the middle of the century, there were more millionaires living in Broughty Ferry per head of population than anywhere else in Europe.

173

Time Tram Dundee

Dundee's Population Explodes

Just over 10,000 people lived in Dundee at the start of the 19th century. During the next eighty years, that figure doubled, tripled, quadrupled and then just plain exploded.

The growing linen industry brought folk in from Fife, Angus and the Highlands of Scotland. By 1821, Dundee's population was around the 26,000 mark.

Then the trade in jute went through the roof and the mill owners needed more workers to keep up with the demand. When word got out that the Dundee textile industry was booming, people came from England, Germany, Italy and Russia to get jobs.

But it was the hard life in another country, Ireland, that really changed the size and shape of the town. Driven by hunger and poverty, tens of thousands of Irish folk left home to find a better future in the mills of Dundee. And by 1881, Dundee's population had jumped to a whopping 140,000.

Folk had the jobs they wanted, the mill owners were making huge fortunes but things in Dundee were far from rosy.

Although some grand new buildings like the Town House and the Trades Hall had been built, Dundee was still a medieval town. Its tiny ancient streets just couldn't cope with the massive increase in population. There were no housing schemes like Ardler, Whitfield, Mid Craigie, Kirkton or Menzieshill in those days. Most people lived in three-hundred-year-old houses or badly-made tenements quickly thrown up by the mill owners. And with almost everyone squeezed in to a handful of streets in the middle of the town, Dundee was the perfect place for a virus to spread.

Some folk slept in windowless rooms. Houses had no running water and it was common for several families to share a single outside toilet. The Plague that killed so many Dundonians in the Middle Ages did not return but other dreadful diseases ran riot in the overcrowded tenements. Outbreaks of cholera, smallpox, typhus, measles and scarlet fever claimed the lives of many people, especially children.

Mary Slessor, Queen of Calabar

Mary Slessor was one tough cookie.

At the age of 27, Mary left her job as a mill worker in Dundee. Already caring for the bairns of the poor in the city's Cowgate, she decided she would go to Africa to become a Christian missionary.

Mary was not choosing an easy life for herself. Missionaries had to travel to a faraway country (usually a very hot one with snakes and crocodiles in it and no flush toilets) and convince the people there to believe in a Christian God and teach them to be nice to everybody.

In Calabar (now Nigeria) where Mary was posted, few believed in God and the people were nice to hardly anybody. Calabar was a dangerous place. If you weren't killed in one of the many wars that afflicted the area, you could be kidnapped, sold into slavery and have to be someone's slave and wash their dishes and polish their shoes for the rest of your life.

Five foot nothing and armed only with a bible and an umbrella, Mary would often stand between two tribes of warriors and tell them off. Occasionally she would hit them with her brolly.

One time she walked eight hours through the jungle to heal a sick chief who thought he was dying, just as the tribe were sharpening the sacrificial knives getting ready to bump off his entire family.

Mary Slessor was frightened of nothing. Travelling on the river one day, her canoe was attacked by an angry hippo and Mary saved everyone on the boat by wedging a big pot in the hippo's mouth.

Mary's strength and courage saved many lives. She worked even harder than she had in the Dundee mills to help the local African children.

In Calabar many people were superstitious and some of their beliefs made them do cruel things. If twins were born, people said it was the work of the devil and they took the babies out to the jungle and left them there to die. Mary simply went round picking the children up off the ground and bringing them home with her.

When she died at the age of 66 in 1915, she was known as the 'Queen of Calabar' but to all the thousands of people that she

Mary Slessor
1848–1915

helped she was just 'Ma'. There are very few statues of Mary Slessor in Scotland but you can see her any time you want on the back of every Clydesdale Bank £10 note.

Life on the Mars

If you misbehave these days, you might be told off or sent to your room. If it's really bad, you might get grounded.

But in the 19th century, there was a chance you would be packed off to live on an old warship in the middle of the River Tay where you would be woken every morning at six by a bugle and ordered to scrub the decks in your bare feet.

The *Mars* was a ship moored just off Newport in Fife. Boys who got themselves into trouble with the police were put there to keep them from getting into even more trouble. Aged between nine and fifteen, the lads received an education, naval training and a good hard clip round the lug-hole if they stepped out of line.

The Mars Training Ship

Dundee's Newspapers

Most Dundonians today get their news from *The Courier* or the *Evening Telegraph*. They keep Dundee folk in touch with all that's happening in the city and around the world.

In the 19th century, the *Dundee Advertiser* was one of many newspapers published in Dundee. But in 1851, a man called John Leng became its editor and turned it into the top newspaper in town. (It later joined with the *Dundee Courier* to become the *Dundee Courier and Advertiser*.)

John Leng then started another paper, the *People's Journal*, which was an even bigger hit. In 1875, the *People's Journal* was selling 130,000 copies a week across the whole of Scotland. Then the *People's Friend* appeared, followed in 1877 by the *Evening Telegraph* which most Dundonians affectionately call the 'Tully'.

Finding time to become a Member of Parliament in 1889, he also set up a singing competition for Dundee school children, known as the Leng medal.

Published today by D.C. Thomson & Co. Ltd, Dundee's papers have been bringing the news to the people for over two hundred years.

The Tay Whale

In December 1883, a large Humpback Whale happened to swim into the Firth of Tay.

Stuck in port for the winter with no chance of making any money from whaling until the spring, the eyes of 700 Dundee whalers lit up. Here was a big beautiful oily whale delivering itself right to their doorstep.

But the Humpback Whale which entered the Tay looking for some fish to nibble was no push over. The Dundee men who sailed out to catch him didn't know what they were letting themselves in for.

After several weeks of following the creature about in small boats, they managed to hit it with harpoons. But the long sharp spears jagging into its side didn't seem to bother it much. Instead the whale swam off at high speed, dragging two row boats, a steam boat and a tug all the way to Montrose, 30 miles north of Dundee. At Montrose, the wind changed direction and the whalers' ropes snapped. The whale broke free, only to be found dead floating off the coast a few days later.

Thousands gathered to see this remarkable beast brought in to Dundee harbour. Its fate lay in one of the town's boiling yards but even in death the whale didn't go quietly.

When its body was lifted up by crane, its tongue, weighing half a ton, fell out of its mouth and crashed down onto the dock. And when the men from the boiling yard came to collect it, the whale's heavy carcass crushed first one lorry, then a second. It finally took an extra strong truck and twenty horses twenty-six hours to transport it just half a mile. The skeleton of the famous Tay Whale was put on display in the city's museum.

The Longest Bridge in the World

Tough luck if you wanted to cross the River Tay by bridge at Dundee before 1870. Anybody needing to cross to Fife had to either
a) take a ferry,
b) walk all the way round by Perth,
c) hitch a ride on the back of a seal or
d) swim for it.

And it was dead slow and stop for trains travelling from Edinburgh to Dundee. To cross the Tay, they had to unhook the train's engine, roll their heavy wagons onto a special ferry called a 'flying bridge', sail across the river and then hitch the wagons up to another engine on the other side. And they had to go through the same rigmarole in order to cross the Forth as well.

The jute mill owners and the North British Railway company had finally had enough of flying bridges. They wanted a real one.

In 1871, under the watchful gaze and huge beard of the engineer Thomas Bouch, a line of little islands began to appear in the River Tay.

Each island had two iron columns. Their job was to hold the bridge up. But first men had to climb down inside them and dig out tons of sand. This made the columns sit more firmly on the river bed. It was risky work though. In 1873, five men drowned at the bottom of one of the metal columns when a wall burst letting in the cold waters of the Tay.

Towers of brick and iron rose up from these man-made islands. Eighty five spans (or little bridges) joined the towers together. A single track railway line was then laid across them from Magdalen Green to Woodhaven in Fife, a distance of almost two miles.

In the middle, trains passed through a long metal cage known as the High Girders. This part of the bridge was higher than the rest so that ships could go under it and up the river to Perth.

It took six hundred men six years to build the first Tay Rail Bridge. When it was opened in 1878, Thomas Bouch's bridge was the longest in the world – and one of the most famous. Queens, presidents and emperors came to Dundee to see the amazing bridge over the Tay. It was thought a marvel of the modern age.

Unfortunately, it wasn't all that marvellous.

Cracks had been appearing in the iron columns for some time. And train drivers racing too fast across the bridge to beat the ferries only made things worse. Apart from a farmer called Patrick Matthew who foretold a terrible disaster, no-one really believed that the bridge could fall down.

And then one stormy night, the bridge fell down.

The Tay Bridge Disaster

Just after seven in the evening on Sunday 28th of December 1879, a train crossing the Tay Bridge disappeared during a violent storm. The 5.27 Burntisland to Dundee train was travelling through the High Girders at top speed when the columns holding up that part of the bridge suddenly collapsed. The engine and carriages fell eighty feet into the raging waters below, killing all seventy five passengers and crew.

William McGonagall famously wrote a poem about the Tay Rail Bridge Disaster. (A lot of people thought his poetry was a bit of a disaster too.)

> *'Beautiful Railway Bridge of the Silv'ry Tay!*
> *Alas! I am very sorry to say...'*

A second bridge was soon built. It has been carrying trains safely over the River Tay since 1887. But if you look closely, you will see next to it the stumps of the old bridge that fell on that terrible winter's night.

185

Dundee Demolition

Dundee's Fish Street no longer exists. It got flattened in 1878 and Whitehall Crescent was built over the top of it.

Although in its last years it had lost a bit of its glamour, Fish Street was formerly one of the best addresses in town. Queen Margaret's ancient palace once stood nearby and Earl David of Huntingdon's house was round the corner. But when Dundee's well-to-do moved out to Broughty Ferry and the West End in the 19th century, Fish Street became home to some of the city's poorest folk.

Narrow lanes, known as wynds, ran down to Fish Street from the Nethergate. When the townsfolk laid out these wynds in the Middle Ages, they made them deliberately crooked to stop the wind blowing into town straight off the sea.

But this labyrinth of winding streets and crooked closes was in the way of progress. Horses and carts had trouble getting in and out of the busy harbour. And the local stone which the houses were made from was dirty and crumbling. Fish Street and many others in Dundee were cleared away by the end of the century.

Provost Pierson's Mansion was knocked down in the 1890s

Couttie's Wynd Up

One street which wasn't demolished was Couttie's Wynd. It's not much to look at these days but this centuries-old thoroughfare still runs between Whitehall Crescent and the Nethergate. A strange tale is told about how it got its name.

Long ago, a Dundee man called Couttie was out in the countryside tending his cattle. When a mysterious stranger wandered by and asked if he could keep him company, Couttie said, 'Eh, nae bather'. But the two men were attacked by bandits and a big fight started. They fought the robbers off, although it was Couttie's dog that did most of the fighting. The mystery man turned out to be King James V of Scotland. As a thank-you present, the king gave his new pal, Couttie, a street in Dundee.

Discovery

In 1899, Sir Clements Markham came to Dundee to buy a ship which could carry men down to the bottom of the world.

As President of the National Antarctic Expedition, Sir Clements knew that Dundee had been building ships to hunt whales for years. They were strong, wooden and pretty much unsinkable – exactly what was needed for sending explorers to the frozen wilderness of Antarctica.

So Sir Clements ordered one and the Dundee Shipbuilding Company got to work putting together the toughest ship ever made – the *Discovery.*

Discovery being freed from the ice

172 feet long, 33 feet wide with 25-inch thick sides and room for 50 men, *Discovery* was launched on 21st of March 1901.

Under the command of explorer Captain Robert Falcon Scott, *Discovery* reached Antarctica in 1902 – but the ship got stuck in ice almost immediately at McMurdo Sound where it lay frozen solid for two long years. Eventually the crew had to blow the ice up with dynamite to get the ship out. (Sadly, Captain Scott died in 1912 trying to reach the South Pole on another expedition with the Dundee ship *Terra Nova*.)

Since leaving Dundee in 1901, *Discovery* has sailed hundreds of thousands of miles around the world. Now she is back in her home port. You can pay her a visit at **Discovery Point** and find out what it was like to journey to the ends of the earth in this famous old ship.

Dundee's Bright Sparks

James Chalmers was a Dundee bookseller who reckoned the postal system was a bit daft. If the postie came to your house, you had to pay *him* for the letter he was delivering – even if it was from someone you didn't like.

So in 1834 James Chalmers thought of a way round this. Why not, he said, get people to buy a stamp first if they want to send a letter? And he made it sticky so it didn't fall off. Hey presto, this bright spark had just invented the adhesive postage stamp.

James Chalmers, 1782–1853

189

While Chalmers was sorting out the postal service, **James Bowman Lindsay** was busy changing the shape of the modern world.

James Bowman Lindsay
1799–1862

In his day job, he was a weaver but his second job was being a genius. When James was born in 1799, no-one had electric light bulbs in their houses. Rooms were lit with gas lanterns, oil lamps or candles. These were smelly, greasy and could burn your house down in about 10 minutes flat.

But in 1835 James Bowman Lindsay showed that an electric light bulb could illuminate a whole room. Next he worked out how to send telegraphic messages through water. Then for fun he wrote a dictionary which contained words from 107 different languages.

Preston Watson
1880–1915

Preston Watson was a daring young Dundonian who wasn't afraid of heights. When he was a wee boy, he believed that one day people would fly like the birds and he built his own glider to prove it.

Early in the 20th century, Preston tied a rope round a tree with his glider at one end and a heavy blacksmith's anvil at the other. When he let go of the rope, the anvil came crashing to the ground but the glider, with Preston in it, skipped lightly into the air. For a few short seconds, Preston Watson was flying.

trehin

flehin

nearly dehin trehin

Dundee Yesterday, Today and Tomorrow

Dundee's Ain

Like other Scottish cities, the Great War (1914 – 1918) touched the lives of the people of Dundee. Great Britain was at war with Germany and millions of men died on the battlefields of Belgium and France.

Based in the city, the Fourth Battalion of the Black Watch Regiment was made up of mostly local men who worked in the town's jute and marmalade factories. Almost everyone had a friend or relative serving in what was known as 'Dundee's Ain'.

In February 1915, the Fourth Battalion was sent to join the fighting in France. A huge crowd of friends and relatives packed Dundee railway station to wave off the battalion's 400 men.

Many of those young soldiers were killed just a few weeks later at the Battle of Neuve-Chapelle but worse was to come.

On 25th of September 1915, Dundee's Ain fought in a fierce battle at a place called Loos in northern France. Among the many casualties, 235 men from the Dundee battalion were wounded or killed.

Every year on that day the beacon on the War Memorial on Dundee Law is lit and we remember the brave men of the

Dundee Law War Memorial

Fourth Battalion who fought and died for their country and their ain hame toun.

Dundee's Cinemas

Long before people had televisions on all day in every room in the house, Dundonians went to the pictures.

In the first half of the 20th century, Dundee had more than 30 cinemas with fancy names like La Scala, Capitol, Rialto, and Tivoli and some not so fancy like Kinnaird, Stobswell and Shand's.

At one point, Dundee boasted the second biggest cinema in Europe, Green's Playhouse in the Nethergate, which had a bums-on-seats capacity of 4,126.

Dundonians loved going to the cinema. Children packed them out on Saturday mornings to watch cartoons. Adults hurried into the picture houses straight from their work. Often the entire family (babies and grannies and all) would go to sit in the dark, munch fish suppers, throw sweeties about, knit, stamp their feet when the film projector broke down and watch the stars of the day on one of Dundee's many silver screens.

Time Tram's Planet Futba

Dundee Football Club

Founded: 1893

Stadium: Dens Park

Capacity: 12,000

Scottish Cup Winners: 1910

Scottish League Champions: 1961-62.

European Cup: semi-finalists, 1963

All-time top scorer: Alan Gilzean

Most successful manager: Bob Shankly

Most famous signing: Claudio Caniggia (Argentina)

Nicknames: the Dark Blues, the Dees.

Dundee United Football Club

Founded: 1909 as Dundee Hibernian
(name changed to Dundee United in 1923)

Stadium: Tannadice

Capacity: 14,000

Scottish Cup Winners: 1994

Scottish League Champions: 1982-83

Scottish League Cup Winners: 1979–80, 1980–81

European Cup: semi-finalists, 1984

UEFA Cup: finalists, 1987

All-time top scorer: Peter McKay

Most successful manager: Jim McLean

Most expensive transfer: Duncan Ferguson to Rangers in 1993
for £4m

Nicknames: the Terrors, the Arabs (nickname for the fans).

195

Winkie the Wonder Pigeon

On 23rd of February 1942, an RAF bomber crashed into the sea off the coast of Norway. The radio was smashed. The plane was wrecked. All that stood between the four crew men and certain death was a rubber dinghy and two pigeons.

The only chance of a rescue depended on tying messages to the birds' legs, hoping they could fly home in time to raise the alarm.

One pigeon was sent off with a message but (they learned afterwards) disappeared never to be heard of again.

The second pigeon, Winkie, escaped from his cage during the crash and ended up covered in diesel oil. Before the airmen could catch him and tie a message saying 'Mum, Help!' to his leg, Winkie flew up into the air, circled the men sitting helplessly in their dinghy then headed off into the distance. The crew at that point must have thought they had had it.

A few hours and hundreds of miles later, Winkie arrived home at his pigeon loft in Long Lane at Broughty Ferry. His owner, George Ross, realising something was wrong, immediately contacted the airbase at RAF Leuchars in Fife. Going by how far and how fast Winkie could fly, they were able to work out quickly where the bomber had crashed. After 22 hours in the water, the bomber crew was rescued, all thanks to Winkie the wonder pigeon, who went on to receive the Dickin Medal.

super doo

Dundee's Comic Geniuses

For generations, children and adults have been splitting their sides laughing at the antics of characters in the *Dandy* and the *Beano*. Although many brilliant creative people have worked on these over the years, here are three of the comic masterminds behind D.C. Thomson.

D.C. Thomson
1861–1954

David Couper Thomson founded D.C. Thomson in 1905. He turned a local newspaper business into a worldwide empire which went on to sell millions of newspapers, magazines and, of course, comics.

R.D. Low
1895–1980

Robert Duncan Low launched D.C. Thomson's most successful comics. His hits include adventure story titles such as the *Hotspur* and comics like the *Dandy* and the *Beano*. He even found time to create the idea behind the Broons and Oor Wullie.

Dudley D. Watkins
1907–1969

Dudley Dexter Watkins joined D.C. Thomson in 1925. His skill as an artist was spotted by R.D. Low and he was soon the company's star illustrator, drawing characters like Lord Snooty, Oor Wullie, the Broons and a certain cowpoke called Desperate Dan.

Desperate Dan

Desperate Dan made his debut appearance in the very first issue of the *Dandy* on 4th of December 1937. The world's strongest man has been in every single issue and in his time has smashed up trains, hotels, houses and trams.

Just like Dan himself, the *Dandy* is a world-beater. In 1999, it published its 3,007th edition, becoming the record holder for the world's longest running comic.

Oor Wullie was introduced to readers of the *Sunday Post* on 8th of March 1936.

He managed to wreck a tram in his very first episode and has been getting into scrapes ever since.

(The Broons appeared for the first time on the very same day.)

Oor Wullie

Lord Snooty

His lordship made his first appearance in the *Beano* in 1938. With his Aunt Matilda who looked after him and his pals, Big Fat Joe and Swanky Lanky Liz, Snooty entertained generations of children and adults alike until 1990.

Created and drawn by David Law, Dennis the Menace started menacing in the *Beano* in 1951.

He was joined in 1968 by his faithful pet dog and fellow menace, Gnasher.

Dennis, who is over 50 years old but still looks about 10, has his own international fan club with one and a half million junior menaces in it.

Dennis the Menace

Dundee Around the World

Dundee is twinned with seven other cities around the world. (If a city has a twin town, it means that folk from these places can visit each other from time to time to swap business cards, exchange ideas and generally be really good pals.) Dundee's Twin Towns are:

Orleans (France)
Wurzburg (Germany)
Chesterfield (England)
Nablus (The West Bank)
Zadar (Croatia)
Dubai (United Arab Emirates)
Alexandria (Virginia, USA)

More Than One Dundee

Although Dundee (Scotland) is the original, it is not the only town to have that name.

When Dundonians left Scotland to settle in other parts of the world, they couldn't bring the Tay or the Law or Wallace's pie shop with them.

So they wouldn't feel too home-sick, they often named their new town after the place of their birth.

The American states of Michigan, Florida, Ohio and New York all have Dundees. In Canada you'll find one in Ontario and another in Nova Scotia.

Dundee, NY

As well as these there is a South African Dundee, a Jamaican Dundee and, if you don't count the film character Crocodile Dundee, there are two more Dundees in Australia.

Dundee, NSW

The Dundee Time Tram has seen it all – a hundred centuries, seven invasions, multiple massacres, sieges, burnings, bouts of plague, flax, jute, whales, haivers and pehs, and with only a little bit to go before its final stop, you'll know by now that Dundee didn't just appear out of nowhere. As a passenger on the Time Tram, you have seen it grow slowly, messily, sometimes painfully but always steadily, into the modern city that it is today.

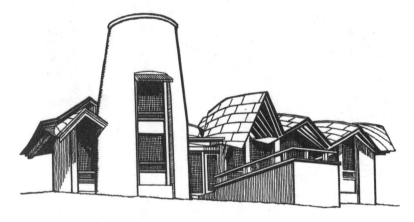

Maggie's Centre

From the first log boats dragged up onto the shore at Seagate to the huge oil rigs which come in regularly to Dundee docks for refitting and repairs, the town's harbour has been the lifeblood of the town.

Medieval townsfolk had to suffer in the awful Sickmen's Yairds but Dundee is now home to internationally renowned medical research laboratories and Maggie's Centre, the city's cutting edge cancer information centre, designed by the famous architect Frank Gehry. With the success of D.C. Thomson's characters like 'Dennis the Menace', the local talent inspiring the worldwide computer games industry and the artwork and drama showcased at the DCA and the Rep Theatre, Dundee's reputation as a creative city continues to grow.

Davie certainly knows one or two things about Dundee he didn't know before. Eh Ken the Seagate seagull is bound to be more unbearable than ever. And hopefully you've picked up some new facts along the way too.

So if you were one of those folk who thought that Dundee was dead boring, maybe you've changed your mind. Maybe now you'll think a bit more about Dundee and its past. And if you're lucky enough to be from Dundee, maybe you'll walk a little bit taller knowing that you come from such an interesting place.

The Last Tram

Dundee folk loved their trams.

The first trams, pulled by horses, were in service in 1877 but by 1902, the trams had gone electric.

For eighty years, tram cars criss-crossed the city, rattling up and down the Hilltown and taking Dundonians to Stobswell, Downfield, Lochee, Broughty Ferry and back again.

Dundee's love affair with the tram car was cut short when they were all replaced by buses in the 1950s. Hundreds of people walked behind Dundee's last tram on its final journey from Maryfield to Lochee on 27th of October 1956.

Have a look at the pavement in the Murraygate to see if you can spot Dundee's last remaining tram tracks.

You never know, you might even see the Dundee Time Tram on another trip through this town's amazing history.

A Note To Our Readers

You might have noticed that in this book, height and distance measurements are given in *feet* or *miles*.

For example –
Glaciers *'two miles high'*
The Law *'571 foot high'*
The Old Steeple *'160 feet high'*

A *foot* (plural *feet*) is the name of a unit of length which was used in Dundee – and all over Britain – before metric units of measurement were introduced to this country.

There are 3 **feet** in a **yard**, and 12 **inches** in a **foot**
1 **foot** = 0.3048 of a **metre** or 30.48 **centimetres**
A **mile** is 1760 **yards** (or 5,280 **feet** or 63,360 **inches**)
1 **mile** = 1609 **metres**, or 1.609 **kilometres**

So, you can do sums and figure out that–
Glaciers *'two miles high'* are *3.218 kilometres high*
The Law *'571 foot high'* is *174.041 metres high*
The Old Steeple *'160 feet high'* is *48.768 metres high*
You could work out–
How many metres long was the Law railway tunnel?
How many centimetres tall was Mary Slessor?
What length in metres was The Discovery?